Also by Lanny Bassham

Freedom Flight - The Origins of Mental Power

With Winning in Mind 3rd. ED.

Cover Photo

Lanny with his twin sons Brian and Troy. Both won full-ride athletic scholarships to college, made All-American in NCAA Rifle and competed for the USA in world competition. Both are Master Level Instructors at Mental Management Systems.

PARENTING CHAMPIONS

WHAT PARENTS NEED TO KNOW ABOUT THE MENTAL GAME

Mental Management® Systems, LLC
700 Parker Square Suite 140
Flower Mound, Texas 75028
972.899.9640
www.mentalmanagement.com

PARENTING CHAMPIONS
WHAT PARENTS NEED TO KNOW ABOUT THE MENTAL GAME

LANNY BASSHAM

Olympic Gold Medalist, World Champion
Founder of Mental Management® Systems.

Dedication

This book is dedicated to the difference makers in our lives, to those who pave the roads so our travel is easier, to those who by their example show us the way, to those who suffer so we do not have to, and to those who have given their lives so we might be free. To the Son of Man for making all things possible. To our fathers and mothers who take the time to listen, to advise, to encourage, to console, to empower, to love and to sacrifice so we might find our way, we give you our thanks.

Introduction

Ask any elite athlete what percentage of their sport is mental, and you will get a huge number back. The statement I hear most often is "My game is 90% mental!" Now, I ask the second question. "If your game is 90% mental, what percentage of your time and money have you spent learning mental skills?" The answer I receive most often is 5 to 10%. Now that just doesn't make sense. The thing that is most important is the thing that we tend to ignore.

If the mental game is so important where are the mental coaches in our schools? There are plenty of technical coaches on the football field. Every team from baseball to track has a coach for technique. There are golf pros and tennis pros in every country club that can teach you to swing the club and the racquet. But where are the mental coaches? They are hard to find, you might think, but you would be mistaken. In fact, they are everywhere. They are the first person the young athlete talks to after the game or practice. They are in the stands, shouting encouragement. They share the joy in every win and the pain in each loss. The most important mental coach in every athlete's life is the parent that drives them home from the game.

Parents are unprepared for the job, and though they love their children, they will likely do more harm than good as their mental coach. But that will not happen to you if you read on and implement the principles of this book. I plan to make you a skilled mental coach for the sake of your children. You are about to learn about Mental Management®. Prepare to be enlightened and empowered.

-Lanny Bassham

Contents

Foreword

As a parent, former high school coach, and with over 40 years as an educator, I believe that Lanny Bassham has hit the target dead center with this seminal work for Parenting Champions. When put into action by parents, these groundbreaking principles will have a positive influence on many young lives now and well into the future. Parents desiring to build champions in their families can't miss when incorporating Lanny's work into the lives of their children.

A child's first and foremost teacher in life will be his or her parents. Unfortunately, there are no instructional manuals on how to parent champions, until now. Based on years of research, Lanny discovered the secrets of winners. This discovery of what winners know and do, that others do not, is the basis for his plan and process for Parenting Champions.

Every parent wants the best for their children; however, our children must live in and navigate a very negative landscape as they grow through life's experiences. At every turn, our children are bombarded with negativity, both in word and action. This negativity suppresses less than stellar growth toward becoming the champion they or their parents wish they could become.

Even well-intentioned parents contribute to the barrage of negativity, which limits growth and progress toward becoming a winner. It seems at every youth athletic event, young girls and boys hear and witness the constant reinforcement that they or a peer is just not good enough. With these negative comments flowing into a child's formative brain they soon succumb to it all and develop a fixed mindset that becomes a self-fulfilling prophecy. A self-fulfilling prophecy that says, I am not good enough and never will be.

Now for some examples, recently I was sitting on the patio of our neighborhood golf clubhouse and witnessed what I assume was a well-meaning father belittle his son over and over regarding his approach shot to the 18th green. From my vantage point, I repeatedly heard the father make negative remarks about his son's performance. Asking him to repeat the shot, the father picked up another golf ball and hurled it back to his son, shouting out his disdain for the shot. After several attempts by his son to improve and the father's response to the shot of, "Do it again," the father, on what would be the last attempt, simply threw the ball in a different direction of his son. Then, he got in the golf cart and headed to the clubhouse leaving his son standing alone on the fairway. Also, I once observed a middle school basketball coach yell, "You couldn't hit the broadside of a barn" as a 7th-grade athlete took a shot missing the backboard. Basketball was a game the young man loved, but he never picked up a basketball again in an organized sports setting. Lanny's work would indicate, those types of statements not only can but most likely will shape the lives of these young people forever. Perhaps if the father and coach in the examples above had had Lanny's book, these situations could have been avoided.

Parents can turn the tide by learning the methods to create the mental side of the game for their children before it might be too late. Mental Management is the key that unlocks the door of becoming a champion. As Lanny reports, 90% of the game is mental; however, many will spend a small percentage on developing the mental side of the game, if any time at all. Parents can turn the tide for their children by learning and deploying the concepts taught by Lanny Bassham, the master of the mental game. The very principles of Mental Management used by athletes from around the world are contained in these pages.

What our children need is what Lanny offers in this book, Parenting Champions: What Parents Need to Know about the Mental Game. Can you imagine the possibilities of a child being nurtured in a 360° environment where teachers, coaches, and parents came together to help young people excel at developing their mental game and becoming champions? In this environment teachers, coaches, parents, and even the child herself or himself sends a consistent and constant mental image in keeping with what one can become by following the principles of Mental Management.

Parents who read this book, study the concepts and principles of Mental Management contained in these pages, and put them into practice with their children will begin the process of parenting champions. While not every child will become an Olympic Gold Medalist or a professional athlete, they will all compete, and Lanny's work will empower parents to aid them in becoming champions in life.

Dr. Lowell H. Strike
Superintendent of Schools
Little Elm ISD
Little Elm, TX

Chapter 1
The Question

I am making the assumption that if you are reading this book, you are most likely a parent. It is also a good possibility that your children are currently competing or will one day become competitors. They will find that life is one big competition. They might compete for a spot on a team, for a role in a school play, for a chair in the orchestra, or a place at the top of the leaderboard. The importance of accomplishment increases as our children mature. When score starts to matter to them, they will soon learn that not everyone wins. Not everyone gets an A. Life is full of B, C, D experiences. Competitions are won and lost. Both accomplishment and disappointment characterize experiences. Soon they will develop an opinion about where they fit in the game. This view or Self-Image, as I choose to call it, will shape their decisions, form their habits and attitudes and determine the course of their lives.

Concerning your kids, I have just one question for you. What is more important to you, what your children Accomplish or who they Become?

I have asked that question to thousands of parents always receiving the same answer. It is who they Become. This response is interesting because in our world Becoming is rarely rewarded, while Accomplishment reigns supreme. Accomplishment is being named a starter on the team. It is the Valedictorian, the All-American, the MVP, and the World Champion. It is your grade in school. If you have an A, you are outstanding, while a C means you are average. It is Gold, Silver, and Bronze in the Olympic Games. It is how much money you earn. Accomplishment is the measurement of your results.

I believe Accomplishment is so often rewarded because it always has a number associated with it. It is easy to measure something if it has a value that is comparable to another value. Score decides grades. Score wins games. Times or points award Olympic medals. Vote count determines elections. Success is often measured by sales figures or profits earned. Accomplishment is rewarded so often because it is easy to measure, not because it is more important than Becoming.

Becoming is often overlooked because it's hard to measure. Becoming is who you are, and there is no easy way to put a number on it. Here is an example. Two men accomplish earning a million dollars in a calendar year, but they make money in different ways. One man bought a business, made mistakes but learning from them, made better decisions and finally sold his business for a million dollars. The other man bought a winning lottery ticket. Both of them accomplished earning a million dollars, but only one of them became anything in the process. What are the chances of the business owner doing it again? Pretty good I'd say. The businessman became something. He became a successful entrepreneur. Becoming is acquiring knowledge, implementing it, and knowing why and how it works to apply it again. Becoming is integrity, character, and confidence. Try to put a number on that.

So, if who your children become is more important to you than what they accomplish, doesn't it make sense to place a high value on Becoming? You can bet the world is doing just the opposite.

It appears that most people today desire winning, fame, and making money more than who they are Becoming. Win at all cost. The end justifies the means. Cheat, if you have to, just don't get caught. You do not have to look far to see examples of this. In fencing, points are signaled by a light that indicates contact made by the opponent's blade. In the Modern Pentathlon event at the 1976 Olympic Games, Boris Onischenko's light went off without explanation during the fencing portion. Something wasn't right. It turned out the Soviet was using a device in his épée's grip to activate the light manually. The athlete was expelled from the games. Onischenko was a Russian grand master of sport, the secretary-general of the Russian Pentathlon Federation, twice national champion, an Olympic Silver medalist in 1972, and a member of the national team that won the gold medal in Munich. No one but Boris Onischenko knows if his previous medals were won fairly. The first problem with cheating is all of the accolades received leading up to being found out pale in comparison to the feeling the winner who wins fairly receives. Secondly, the cheater knows he has accomplished nothing by cheating, but he has become something. He has become a cheat.

I wish to make my point as forcefully as possible.

"What your children accomplish only affects what they do today. Who they become affects all of their actions in the future."

I am not against winning but winning is very temporary. For a short time after a win, you are a rock star, a big deal, and admired by all. But, at the next event, you do not get extra points for having won the previous one. Becoming, on the other hand, is long lasting. It is currency you can spend over and over and still have it to use again.

We become by overcoming. It is rarely learned when everything goes without a hitch. We become when we encounter obstacles that stand in our way and force us to get better or smarter to get beyond them. Have you ever competed in an event and did not score well but learned a ton? The fact that you learned something new is becoming. Becoming is finishing the game stronger than you were when you began.

Attainment, now that's a word you don't hear used every day. It's a special one because it includes not only what you accomplished but also the way you accomplished it. Here at Mental Management System, we are so fond of this concept that my son Troy wrote a book called *Attainment - The 12 Elements of Elite Performance*. Attainment is both becoming and accomplishing.

Accomplishing is how we measure the External.

Becoming is how we measure the Internal.

Attainment = Accomplishing + Becoming

What seems to be lacking in the world's volume of work on performance improvement, in my humble opinion, is a different way of describing what those of us that compete are striving to do. We are not only seeking to win. We are also seeking to discover. We not only want to get to the top of the mountain we want to strengthen physically, mentally, and spiritually because of the climb. We are seeking to become something different than what we were when we started the struggle. We are seeking Attainment.

Athletes know that scores are not the only way to measure improvement. It's common to hear a performer say, "I scored well, but it didn't feel that good." or "I feel I performed much better today than my place indicated." Score only measures the accomplishment.

*"Where you finish does not always measure
how far you've come."*

It is not a question of if you will have to overcome but when. As the great U.C.L.A basketball coach John Wooden once said, "Why do we dread adversity when we know that facing it is the only way to become stronger, smarter, and better?" The difference between accomplishing and attaining is the personal growth part of the journey to the goal. It's the becoming of something better or greater. All too often we as parents are focused only on the accomplishing, forgetting that it is who are children are becoming that is most important.

Chapter 2
My Story

I was in sixth grade, and we were studying the Olympics in school. The teacher said, "You know it is possible that someone in this class might become Olympic Champion someday. I wonder who would have the best chance in the class?" A boy sitting next to me jumped right up and said, "Teacher, I don't know who would have the best chance, but I know for certain who would have the worst chance, Lanny!"

I was the worst athlete in school, and I can prove it. I played second-string right field in Little League baseball. In Little League, right field is where you put your worst player, and I was the alternate. I was short, slow, and uncoordinated so perhaps this comment was well deserved, but it still hurt.

My father was a military officer and a war hero. As an only child, I wanted more than anything to make him proud of me. After playing poorly in a ball game, I remember telling him, "I'm sorry, Dad. I'm just no good." He said, "No, you're mistaken. There is nothing wrong with you, son. You just haven't found what you are good at yet. Keep looking." One day a friend of mine invited me to a rifle club meeting.

"What do you do at a rifle club meeting?" I asked.

"We shoot rifles. It's fun, and it's an Olympic sport," he said. I was interested.

"How strong do you have to be to be a rifle shooter?" I asked.

"You don't have to be strong. The rifles aren't that heavy." He said.

"How tall do you have to be to be a rifle shooter?"

"You don't have to be tall."

"OK, how fast do you have to be to be a rifle shooter?"

"You don't understand." He replied. "You don't have to be tall or strong or fast. All you have to do to be the best rifle shooter in the world is stand still."

"Great!" I exclaimed. "There's an Olympic sport where all you have to do is be still. I can do that. I've had lots of practice in right field."

My father took me to that rifle club meeting, and they let me shoot. I wasn't good at it, but I wasn't bad at it. I was average. I had never been average at anything in my life, and I was average at this sport from the very first night. Shooting was all I talked about the next week. My dad took me to the next meeting, but when we arrived, the man running the club gathered us around and explained that he had some bad news.

"I'm afraid we are not going to be able to shoot tonight. In fact, we are not going to be shooting at all. We have some trouble with using this range, and tonight is our last night." Walking out of the range with my father, I remember looking up at him.

"You know Dad. I think this is the most disappointed I have been in my life!"

Then my father said, "I don't want you to worry about this, son. I'll take care of it. I'm your dad. I'll pick you up from school tomorrow." The next afternoon, my father was waiting for me after school. In the back seat of our car was all the equipment needed to shoot. He'd arranged the use of an indoor shooting hall, and for the next year, he taught me to shoot. He encouraged me, became my coach, and took up the sport as well. We practiced together and became a team. He and I became best friends on that rifle range. Fifteen months after beginning shooting, I won my first national championship.

I don't think I had any special ability for shooting, but I did have several things in my favor. First, my father was a solution-based coach. There are two kinds of coaches in the world. A problem-based coach is quick to say, "Here is what you are doing wrong." He tends to focus on the problem and not so much on the solution to the problem. My father once told me, "Son, there is only one best way to do anything. We are going to learn everything we can about that one best way." If I shot a bad shot, he would not tell me what I did wrong. Instead, he would always say, "Here's what you need to do." Everything was solution based with my father. I would learn later that every time I pictured a solution to a shot, my Self-Image was growing. We did not know the term Self-Image, but somehow my father knew that talking about the solution was better for me than talking about the problem. Every time you think about the problem your Self-Image shrinks.

Additionally, I was blessed with having the range to myself for the first year of my learning to shoot. This was a huge advantage. When you shoot at a club, you have the possibility of people talking about their bad shots and rarely talking about their good ones. I had none of that. I had no other shooters to compare to me. I was not competing, so score was not as important as the process of executing a good shot. I was competing against myself. I could focus without the drama that always occurs with comparing yourself with others.

Finally, I was motivated to the point of passion. When a person is passionate about something training is not something they HAVE to do, it is something they GET to do.

At the beginning of my second year of shooting my father was assigned to the United States Army Marksmanship Unit in Ft. Benning Georgia. The United States dominated international rifle shooting during this period, and the shooters of this unit were the best in the world. Having access to them was a game changer. I remember coming home from school one afternoon to see the current Olympic Gold Medalist, the current World Champion and two former World Champions sitting at my dining room table, eating my mother's chili. All of these shooters had taken ROTC in college, shot on the university rifle team, made All-American and upon entering the Army were assigned to the unit. I followed this pattern and joined the team in the fall of 1969.

During the next three years, I worked hard and moved up the ranks into the top four shooters on the team. I made the World Shooting Championship team in 1970 but did not shoot well at the event.

For the next few years, I struggled to shoot well enough to win. I knew something was wrong, but I did not know what it was. Practicing more often, trying harder, and thinking about winning all of the time did not solve the problem. It was not until I had a mental meltdown in the 1972 Olympics, costing me the Gold Medal, that I knew why I was not winning. I needed a new mental game.

In 1972, there were no seminars in mental training like the one I teach today. Over the next two years, I spent several hours daily gathering information about the mental aspect of sport. I interviewed World and Olympic Champions, asking questions like: "What do you think about when you are performing?" "What makes you able to win when others fail?"

Like the pieces of a puzzle, my mental game started to come together. I created the Mental Management System, and in 1974, I established the U.S. national record of 1179/1200, which stood for more than fourteen years. Also, during the 1974 World Shooting Championships in Switzerland, I won three individual world titles, eight gold medals, and with the assistance of my teammates, I set four world records.

In many ways, I had become a different person. I was confident and in control. I changed mentally. I changed my Self-Image. My habits and attitudes were those of a winner. I had developed a system to control the mental aspects of my performance – The Mental Management® System. Winning became a habit. In 1976 in Montreal, Canada, my lifelong dream came true. I won the Olympic Gold Medal. Then, two years later, I repeated as World Champion in Seoul, South Korea.

I began teaching The Mental Management® System to athletes shortly after the Olympics. I have given seminars on four continents, and the system has been translated into more than a half-dozen languages. I have had as clients the Olympic teams of Great Britain, Japan, Korea, Singapore, Taiwan, India, Canada, Australia, and the United States. I have had the pleasure of presenting The Mental Management® System to Olympic athletes, PGA Tour players, doctors, attorneys, teachers, accountants, business executives, directors of sales, the Navy SEALs, Miss USA winners, Miss America finalists, the FBI, the US Marshals, and even the United States Secret Service. I've had the privilege of helping elite competitors win National, World and Olympic titles with Mental Management®.

I began to realize that our children may be denied reaching their full potential simply because the information they need is not readily available. Secondly, The habits and attitudes necessary for them to be their best must be started while they are young. Waiting until well into adulthood to learn them means mental errors will be reinforced and become embedded making them harder to correct. A Champion Self-Image must be developed as early as possible.

Simply put, the world is designed to keep our children in the middle of the leaderboard. The deck is stacked against them getting anywhere near their true potential in life unless we intervene while they are young. It will be up to us, their parents, coaches, and teachers, to eliminate the primary reason why they will likely fail in reaching the top of their mountain.

By the time our children reach adulthood, they will be carrying so much negative baggage that the sheer weight of it will keep them from reaching the top. I take no delight is saying this, but most of the weight will have been caused by us, the parents.

I have made almost every mistake discussed in this book with our three children. My goal is to inform, not to convict. I trust that much of what I will suggest is well known to you, but I hope in some way to empower you to aid your young performers in becoming all that they can be.

Chapter 3

Reasons for Concern

What is the probability that our children will reach the top of their real potential? Isn't that a primary concern of every parent, teacher, and coach? One way to define winning is you win when you reach the top of your potential. We accept that our children are different and what is the top for one is not the same for everyone. While what it takes to reach the top of one's true potential is not secret, it is hidden. Consider the following.

We are taught if we set high goals, get good technical instruction and work hard it will get us to the top. That is all we have to do. But that is not true. While important, these things will only get you off of the bottom of the leaderboard and to the middle of it. There is a disturbing fact that 95% of all winning is accomplished by only 5% of the participants. If you want your children to get to the top of their potential, they have to know what the top 5% know.

Unfortunately, there are three main reasons why it is improbable they will ever find the essential information that will get them in the top 5%.

1. The people that have the information are usually not able to share it with them.

2. The model that the world presents to them is inadequate.

3. The paramount information will come to them too late.

Learning From Champions

What separates the good from the great? I have made it my life's work to study the top 5% and to write about and teach why they are different from those not in the top. You see, early in my career, I was in the next 5%, just out of the top. I thought if I just learned more, competed more, and outworked my competition, it would pave the way to the top of the leaderboard.

After years of no wins, I realized there was some valuable information hidden from me. I determined that how a champion shot a rifle was no secret because you could see everything related to form. But, you could not see what the champion was thinking, and that made all the difference.

To find the answers it became necessary to ask the winners directly, so for two years; I interviewed Olympic Gold Medalists and World Champions about their mental game. I discovered that most champions are unconsciously competent. They can do it, but cannot tell you how they do it. Their mental game is a black box. The problem with this method is if you find yourself off-center, you may have no way to get back to center. After a while, I began to find top 5% champions that could explain elements of what they were doing and a mental system began to emerge.

I was able to obtain information that was impossible for others to discover. As an Olympic Silver Medalist, I had access to all of the Gold Medalists. I was never turned down for an interview.

You might think that it is a disadvantage for champions to share their secrets. But the exact opposite is often true. It is quite common for winners to talk about their form openly and honestly. I know many World Champions that are also highly regarded technical instructors. It is uncommon, however, for these champions to talk about the thing that they say is 90% of their sport, how they think. It is much easier to demonstrate what they are physically doing than it is to discuss what they are thinking about while they are doing it.

So here is the bottom line. The people that know the mental game information that can move someone from good to great, are either unable to communicate it or unwilling to take the time and effort to master teaching it, choosing to teach form instead.

Learning From the World

*"The world today is designed to keep your
children self-centered instead of self-reliant,
negative instead of positive and entertained
instead of educated."*

One way to evaluate a culture is to look at its role
models. Our culture seems to value fame and riches
over character. If you wish to follow this path becoming takes second place to accomplishment. Not
a good idea you say. The world tends to make decisions based on what's in it for me instead of is this
the right thing to do.

The world of sport is full of negative. Ask any
player, in any sport today, when they come off of the
playing field "How did you do?" and you will hear
them talk about what went wrong first. Your children
hear this and react to it by repeating this habit. Additionally, we live in a world where it is common to not
reward winners because those that do not win might
feel bad. When this happens we discourage excellence by giving everyone a trophy.

Technology is both a blessing and a curse. You
can instantly find anything on the Internet. Anything!
Cell phones and tablets provide instant digital communication and that is a good thing, but they are an
instant available source of entertainment that may
sap productivity if left unchecked.

I am not saying this as a hit on world culture,
but only to remind us that the chance our children

will become productive people of character might be in jeopardy. I am suggesting that some of the things I have learned that have been difference makers in developing World and Olympic Champions are not currently taught in our schools. If kids are going to learn them, they need to be taught by parents.

The Information May Come Too Late

I believe the primary reason people do not reach anything close to their full potential in sport, business, and life is a result of ineffective thinking. We begin making mental mistakes as soon as we start taking up a sport, learning a trade or interacting with society. I believe that most people learn a sport much the same way I did, focusing on form at the expense of mental skills. I've heard people say, "You do not need to worry about the mental game until you have acquired competence in skill training." Nothing could be further from the truth. You must begin to learn mental skills from the beginning. I firmly believe that by learning and using the principles in the following chapters your children can eliminate 75% of all mental error for the rest of their lives.

> *"You should begin to teach practical mental skills to your children when they start to learn physical skills."*

The most common statement our clients make after taking training from us is to say, "I wish I had known this earlier in my career." I can say the same. You cannot wait until your young competitors have experienced years of mental error. It becomes like them to make mistakes, and these mistakes become embedded and difficult to correct. Do not wait until it is too late.

Chapter 4

Phases and Processes

L et's begin to learn the essential information about the mental game that will aid your young competitors in becoming their best. Much of what I am talking about is common sense. In fact, if you read a book and do not recognize any of the concepts in the book at all, the author is dead wrong! I am hoping to take some proven concepts to a deeper and more practical level. Here is an example.

"Every task in life has three phases, the Anticipation Phase, the Action Phase and the Reinforcement Phase."

The Anticipation Phase is what you think about before the action. The Action Phase is what you think about during the action. The Reinforcement Phase is what you think about immediately after the action. The difference between the champion and the average performer lies in the edge the winner gains in the anticipation, action and reinforcement phases of performance. Champions carefully prepare for their tasks, concentrate properly while performing them, and reinforce all good results while correcting errors. It's important to understand what these phases mean so that you'll know how certain techniques I mention later can work for your young performers.

Let's look at some examples. The Smiths are going out to dinner this evening. The Anticipation Phase includes everything leading up to eating the meal, including deciding what restaurant to go to, where to sit at the table and what to order. Eating and drinking make up the Action Phase. The Reinforcement Phase includes evaluating the meal experience and paying the bill and tip. Did the meal meet with satisfaction? Was the food tasty? How about the service and the atmosphere? Was this a positive or a negative experience?

Let's take a sports example. Jeff Smith is on his high school golf team. Every golf shot Jeff hits has these three phases. The Anticipation Phase starts when Jeff begins to gather information about the shot he is about to attempt, including determining his target, which club he will use and a practice swing or two. It also includes his alignment to the ball and target, his grip, and posture. At takeaway, the Action Phase begins, and it ends when his club no longer has contact with the ball. Jeff may think his shot is finished, but the Reinforcement Phase is just beginning.

How Jeff handles his thoughts and actions during the few seconds after his shot is critical. The Anticipation and Action Phases of a shot only determine where the ball lands but the Reinforcement Phase determines who the player becomes and affects all of the shots he will hit for the rest of his life. Is he going to respond or react to this shot? If the result of the shot is negative will Jeff's reaction to it grow him or slow him? Players who do not understand the importance of mental control after a shot tend to react emotionally based on the result of the shot. If the shot is a good one, they are happy but, if the shot is a poor one, most players tend to negatively reinforce the shot by thinking about what they did wrong. We tend to become what we reinforce. Reacting negatively to a bad shot by focusing on the problem and not the solution improves the chances of repeating the error.

My favorite principle of Mental Management addresses this issue.

> *"Every time you think about, talk about*
> *or write about something happening you*
> *improve the probability of it occurring in the*
> *future."*

People in the middle of the leaderboard tend to think about the problem and the adverse effect of the shot on their score. This is reacting to the shot. Instead of thinking about the problem, which improves the chances of more bad shots in the future, try thinking about the solution to the problem. Reinforce what would make it a good shot. This is responding to the shot. Responding instead of reacting teaches becoming. The player is becoming an in-control player on the course. By responding, it is becoming like him to reinforce the solution rather than the problem creating fewer bad shots and is an example of a proper use of the Reinforcement Phase of an task.

Every action has these three phases, but most coaches, teachers, and parents act as if there are only two, the Anticipation Phase and the Action Phase. They act as if the only important thing is the accomplishment of a good score and not who the competitor is becoming in the process. I submit that the world is only interested in what your children accomplish, not in who they become along the way. Reinforcing who they become is your job. If you think this is tough, you are correct. But, if you are serious that becoming is important then you must give this your attention.

People are surprised when I say I am more concerned about what my clients think about after a task than what they think about before a task. What you picture in the Anticipation and Action Phase is critical, but it is not more important than what you think about after the action. The top 5% know this crucial piece of information and use it to great advantage. To successfully help your kids properly use the Reinforcement Phase it is necessary to understand the Conscious, Subconscious and Self-Image.

The Conscious Mind

Performance is a function of three mental processes. The Conscious Mind contains your thoughts and mental pictures. The Conscious Mind controls all of the senses: seeing, hearing, smelling, tasting and touching. Every time we think about something, we do it consciously. The Conscious Mind processes our environment. Its normal function is to gather information and give us options, playing a vital role in our life. Before we can expect to be successful, we first have to consider what type of success we desire. For some of us, winning will have a different meaning. Some people view winning as being the best in a tournament. Others see winning as reaching a personal goal, playing beyond a certain level or beating a particular team. No matter how you define it, we all view winning consciously. We set goals, establish priorities and determine timelines consciously. We think out our life, and that is why it is so important. We tend to move toward what we picture.

These pictures commonly originate from either our environment or our will. We take in information, filter it by our opinions and experiences, and create a thought, taking place without perceptible effort and is almost instantaneous. The environment is doing the creating. One thing separating humans from lower forms of animals is the ability to control what we picture by our will alone. Often, will controlled thoughts are created by us in spite of our environment. Sensory perception tends to dominate our thoughts, but we have the ability to think independently of the world around us if we desire. We can choose to think about the problem or the solution. That choice is made consciously, and will likely determine the fate of your children in sport and life.

The Subconscious Mind

The Subconscious Mind is the source of your skills and power to perform. All great performances are accomplished subconsciously, without much conscious thought. We develop skills through repetition of conscious thought until the Subconscious Mind automatically executes them. In most applications, there are far too many parts moving at one time to think about all of them consciously. This fact explains why most performance applications seem difficult in the beginning. Nevertheless, with hard work and practice, it is possible to master the core competencies needed to grow. Once performers have developed skill and can perform these motions subconsciously, it allows them to start learning advanced skills to take their ability to the next level.

The Self-Image

If you and I are in a playoff against each other, and you think you can beat me, and I think you can beat me, it is over for me. That is Self-Image. The Self-Image makes you "act like you." It is the total of your habits and your attitudes. It is the most important of the three mental processes because the Self-Image and success are directly related. Your performance and your Self-Image are always equal. If you are not content with your current performance level, then your attitude, your habits, or both must change.

The Self-Image and the Conscious Mind are always in communication with one another. Every time we think about something or attempt to do something it creates an imprint and stores it in the Self-Image. The Self-Image generates an attitude on how you see yourself based on these imprints. It determines what is "like you" or "unlike you" to do. We have a Self-Image about everything. It makes us who we are.

The sad thing is that most people believe there is nothing they can do about their Self-Image. They believe that they are the way they are and cannot change. In fact, we are changing all the time. We experience change as we age. The direction of that change can either be determined by you or for you. If you do not take control of your Self-Image, others most surely will. I believe that one of the most important factors in success at the Olympic level is that Olympians tend to control their Self-Image growth.

I believe the current Self-Image of your children is the total of the imprinting they have received during their life. This Self-Image is who your children have become. Who they become in the future will be directly affected by future imprinting. Let's take a look at the kinds of imprints.

Actual Imprints

What happens to us creates an indelible Imprint on the Self-Image. Our lives are full of failures and successes causing our Self-Image to grow and shrink regularly. If your young baseball player gets a hit, it becomes like him to get a hit. If he strikes out, it becomes like him to strike out. These are Actual Imprints, created by the results of our efforts. When we succeed, it becomes like us to succeed, but when we fail, we add an Imprint that it is like us to fail to the pile in our Self-Image.

Fortunately for all of us, what happens is not the only form of imprinting. If this were true, we would never improve. When we begin any new skill, we tend to fail more often than succeed in early attempts. It becomes like us to fail. I remember my first attempt at playing guitar. The strings produced a buzzing noise and the tips of my fingers hurt. Fortunately, my teacher gave me a word of encouragement and motivated me to continue. Another form of imprinting is called an Imagined Imprint.

Imagined Imprints

"There are three kinds of Imagined Imprints, what you picture, what you say and what you write."

Every time you think about something happening it creates an imprint on your Self-Image. Be careful what you think about, as every time you picture something happening you are improving the probability that it will become like you to make it happen. What do your children picture? Every time they worry, it enhances the likelihood that what they are worried about will happen. If they worry about failing an exam, they are imprinting it is like them to fail, and the Self-Image with all its power will move them to make the Imprint a reality. It is not what they want, but it is what they will get if they continue to think this way. You must teach them to picture what they want to happen and not to think about or worry about what they are afraid might happen.

That is good advice for you as well. Your Self-Image is affected by what you picture.

"Whatever you think a thing to be, that's what it becomes."

Also, be careful what you talk about, as I've seen the following situation hundreds of times. Two players meet after a golf competition. John asks Bill, "How did you do?" Bill says, "I did terribly. I had three bogeys in a row. Two were caused by bad tee shots, and the other one came because I ran a putt too long." Bill has just improved the probability of he will bogey holes the same way in the future because he is thinking and talking about his mistakes. His Self-Image is forming the attitude that making bogeys is like Bill. He is becoming what he is Imprinting.

It is unfortunate John is listening to Bill, as he is also improving the chance that he will have Bill's problems in the future. Do not spend time listening to the problems of others, or you will soon inherit their problems.

It has been my observation that Olympians tend to talk less about what they did and much more about what they need to do. Thinking about problems will keep you in the middle of the leaderboard. You must only reflect on the solutions to the problems.

"Every time you picture a problem your Self-Image shrinks. Picturing solutions cause the Self-Image to grow."

Be careful not to complain. I often hear people in both business and sport, complain about their circumstances. Complaining is negative reinforcement, causing people to become the people about whom they are complaining. Teach your children not to reinforce a bad outcome by thinking and talking about it.

One of the most dominant forms of imprinting is writing. You have probably heard that written goals are more likely to be achieved than unwritten ones. I believe this is true because writing something is a great way to imprint the Self-Image. We teach our clients to keep a performance journal. It is different from a diary where you write down everything that happened, good or bad. Diaries tend to become lack-of-performance journals.

Today kids are writing all of the time, called texting. Every text is a potential imprint. Texts are influencing who your children are becoming. Scary, but true. But this is not all bad. Talking about solutions and writing praising and encouraging texts are good for the Self-Image. Social Networking is a blessing or a curse depending on the way it is used.

Just become aware of what is actually happening to your children's Self-Image when they use social media and technology.

Environmental Imprints

It is probable that the greatest Imprint on your children's Self-Image will come from their environment. If we are around positive people, we tend to be positive. If we are surrounded by lazy people, it saps our motivation. The environment is a powerful influence and teacher.

I wish we lived in a world where the environment was always positive and helpful for Self-Image development. Sadly, this just is not the case. In my more than 39 years as a performance coach, I've seen much more negative than positive among competitors. I often ask my clients before Mental Management training begins, "When competitors ask you how you are doing in your sport, do you tend to talk about what you are doing well or what you are doing poorly?" Most talk about what went wrong more often than what went right. How about your child's activity? When you ask the participants how they are doing, do they talk about what went wrong first? If that is true, then their environment is negatively charged. It is a rare exception to find a group of competitors, a team, a club, a school or a workplace where the environment is more positive than negative. Unfortunately, there is no escape from the imprinting of a negative environment, but you can neutralize it, and I will show you how.

The Relationship

In this chapter, we have discussed the three phases of a task and the three mental processes that control performance. I tend to teach about the processes as if they are circles. The bigger the circles, the better the benefit to the performer. There is a direct relationship between the phases and the processes.

The Anticipation Phase of any task is a Conscious circle issue. The Conscious mind is adept at strategy, goal setting, planning, and rehearsing. These essential elements are performed before the action. The Conscious mind is not so proficient at actually performing the task itself; that is best done by the Subconscious mind.

The Action Phase is a Subconscious circle issue. When players are well training and have developed skill through thousands of repetitions, the Conscious mind needs to get out of the way and let the Subconscious mind do its job.

The Reinforcement Phase, what you think about immediately after the action, is a Self-Image circle issue. Is it like a player to get angry and reinforce an error by thinking or talking about it? The Self-Image imprints most immediately after the action. What your children think about immediately after the Action Phase of a task is shaping their Self-Image for the future.

What you think about in the Anticipation and Action phase of an action only affects the current task. But, what you think about after the action phase is long lasting. These thoughts produce imprints in your Self-Image. It becomes like you to do what you are imprinting. You must aid your young performers to control their imprinting. It is possible to grow a positive Self-Image within a negative environment by choosing how you handle what you decide to imprint after every task.

"What happens to your children in life is not nearly as important as what they do about what happens." -Zig Ziglar

Chapter 5

Principles of Mental Management

The principles of Mental Management® govern how the mind works. These principles are concepts familiar to winners that have stood the test of time. They work for all people all the time and apply to sports performance, business success, and personal development. Remember, you are a mental coach. These principles are priceless in aiding you in helping your young performers become their best.

Principle of Mental Management® Number 1

"The Conscious Mind can only concentrate on one thing at a time."

If you are picturing something positive, it is impossible, at the same time, to picture something negative. And, if you have a negative thought, you cannot, at the same time, think positively.

This is good news because it is impossible to picture playing well and playing poorly at the same time. You are either picturing something that will help you or something that will hurt you. The human mind can control thoughts for short periods of time by personal will alone. What we picture is critical.

I remember a baseball coach telling me, "Whatever you do Bassham, don't strike out!" What do you imagine when you hear, "Don't strike out?" I picture striking out. It is impossible to think about hitting the ball if you are picturing striking out. In golf, for example, it is impossible for you to concentrate on the process of hitting the shot you want and thinking about the outcome at the same time. If your thoughts focus on the score, or where you are on the leaderboard, your performance will suffer. You must keep your mental picture centered on execution, not outcome.

Principle of Mental Management® Number 2

"What you say is not as important as what you cause yourself or others to picture."

This is the fundamental principle of successful communication. What you say is not as important as the image your words convey. When the coach said, "Whatever you do Bassham, DON'T STRIKE OUT!" I pictured striking out. He set me up for failure by the way he talked to me. If he had said, "GO STRIKE OUT!" It would have had the same effect on me. Instead, he should have said, "Bassham, JUST HIT THE BALL!"

Remember, what you say to your kids always

affects the imprinting of their Self-Image. What do you think they are picturing when you talk to them. Whatever it is, that's what they are becoming.

Principle of Mental Management® Number 3

"The Subconscious Mind is the source of all mental power."

When your children begin anything – piano lessons or their first day on the golf course – they have a lot of things to think about because nothing is automated in the beginning and good performance seems difficult. Most things, such as playing music or sports, require them to do many things at the same time. Because the Conscious Mind can only do one thing at a time, first experiences are very frustrating. The Conscious Mind needs assistance, which it gets from a second mental process called the Subconscious Mind.

I define skill as doing something consciously long enough for the process to become automated by the Subconscious Mind. Unlike the Conscious Mind, the Subconscious can do many things at once. In fact, your brain is like a large computer. Just how many separate functions can be handled by the Subconscious simultaneously is difficult to measure, but it may be in the billions. Your Subconscious Mind can perform a high number of activities simultaneously. We need to execute the task in the Subconscious mode rather than the Conscious one because it is vastly more powerful.

Elite gymnasts make their challenging sport "look" easy. If you have ever tried to pull yourself up on the rings, you immediately gain a tremendous amount of respect for the strength needed to be a gymnast. Their skill comes from years of training. Through years of training, the routines become subconsciously automated. I once asked a gymnast on the U.S. team what he thought about when he performed. He answered, "I try to feel the flow of the routine. I do not want to believe that any element is particularly challenging or dangerous while performing." You perform best when you allow your well-trained Subconscious to do the work. However, the Conscious Mind can override the Subconscious. When this happens, performance almost always deteriorates. Sleep is a Subconscious action. If you attempt to override the Subconscious by consciously trying to make yourself GO TO SLEEP NOW, you will probably be up most of the night.

Principle of Mental Management® Number 4

"The Self-Image moves you to do whatever the Conscious Mind is picturing."

Let's look at two examples from my book *With Winning in Mind*.

When my daughter was nine years old, I asked her to carry a cup of coffee to a guest in our house. Then I said, "Don't spill it!" That was a bad thing to tell her. When she spilled the coffee, I should not have been surprised. After all, I put the idea in her mind. It was my error, not hers. When you say, "Don't spill the coffee." what picture is created in the Conscious Mind? I imagine spilling the coffee. The Self-Image moves you to do whatever the Conscious Mind is picturing, and it is picturing spilling the coffee.

It is the same in sports. There are only four seconds left in the game, time for only one more play. A touchdown is needed to win. The coach calls for his best fullback to carry the ball. He explains the play. "Now young man, you are our only hope to win this game. I want you to go out there and take the handoff from the quarterback and run in for the touchdown. You can do it."

In goes the fullback, explaining the play to the quarterback. The quarterback says, "That's great call. We are going to win as long as you don't fumble!"

Being positive is our only hope. Positive pictures demand positive results from the Subconscious. If we think negatively, we have to expect negative results.

Principle of Mental Management® Number 5

"You can replace the Self-Image you have with the Self-Image you desire, thereby enhancing a change in performance."

The problem for most of us, and for our children, is we know something has to change for our lives to improve but we want the change to be in other people, or other things, and not in ourselves.

Change is a difficult enough challenge for adults to face. Think of the what your young performers are going through when you add the transition of growing up into the mix.

Their Self-Image is always changing, and you can help direct the change or simply let their environment make the change without you. Remember, every time you cause your kids to think about an error; you make it like them to repeat it. Every time you cause them to think about a solution to a problem it becomes more like them to solve it.

Concentration is nothing more than the control of one's mental picture. Remember, the Subconscious, with all its power, moves them to do whatever the Conscious Mind programs. If you can control the image, you can control the performance. Our conscious picture is formed from what we think about, talk about, and write.

Tell your children not to reinforce a bad performance by getting angry. Anger tends to increase the power of imprinting. Remember, mistakes are never a mental error if we learn from them.

Principle of Mental Management® Number 6

"The more we think about, talk about and write about something happening, we improve the probability of that thing happening."

The Principle of Reinforcement is my favorite principle of Mental Management®. Every time your kids think about, talk about or write about something happening, they improve the likelihood that it will occur. Every time they worry, they improve the probability that what they are worried about will happen. If they are afraid of failing an exam, they are imprinting that it is like them to fail, and the Self-Image, with all its power, will move them to make the Imprint real.

Positive Prediction: Reinforcement in Advance

People tend to perform as we expect them to perform. There is a technique I call Positive Prediction. It is useful in enhancing both performances and in building character. It is a compliment given in advance of a future action. My father once told me that to obtain what you want, you must first provide someone else what they want. He knew I was motivated by recognition and praise. He would often say things like this.

"I bet if you put your mind to it you could get the lawn mowed this afternoon. I would really like to see it looking good."

"It would make your Mom happy if your room was clean and straighten up. What do you think?"

Mowing the lawn and cleaning my room were my chores but l sometimes needed a little help remembering to do them. When Dad talked this way, causing me to picture what I needed to do, and because I wanted to please my parents, I normally did it. Contrast this with the following,

"I see the lawn is not mowed. Better get on it."

"Why can't you clean up your room? It's a mess."

These commands are not necessarily out of line, but they cause the person receiving them to picture being reprimanded instead of praised. The Self-Image moves us to do what we are picturing, and these comments make it more likely the child will not do them. I don't think parents intend for this to happen. I believe they just don't know that it is going on.

When we implement Positive Prediction correctly, everyone wins. You feel great using the technique. The person you are talking to gets a lift, and the results make everyone feel good.

Praise: Reinforcement After the Fact

Praise good performances, and the good performances will repeat. Here is a tip to increase your rapport with your kid's teachers. The teachers in our local school were exceptionally considerate of my children. I called the school office to set an appointment with each of our child's teachers. When I met them they asked, "Mr. Bassham, why did you wish to see me? Is there a problem?"

"No," I replied, "I just wanted to meet you and say that you are one of the most considerate teachers in the school. I am delighted my child can be in your class. I expect, now that we have met, you will not hesitate to give me a call if there is anything that we can do to aid our child in school."

Teachers rarely hear good news from parent conferences. When they are informed a parent is seeking a meeting, it is almost guaranteed an upset parent is requesting it. It makes their day when someone calls in to compliment rather than complain. I believe if parents made an effort to first meet the teachers of their children in this manner that later potential problems would lessen.

Job one for parents is to say and do things that cause their children to understand when their behavior and attitudes are appropriate or inappropriate and to prepare them to become adults that tend to do the proper thing.

One way for parents to accomplish this is to keep their children focused on the solution and not on the problem.

Focusing on the Solution causes the Self-Image to Grow. Focusing on the Problem causes the Self-Image to Shrink.

I understand that it is often necessary to address the error to move to the solution. But, all too often parents tend to major in the problem and minor in the solution, causing the Self-Image to shrink. Not good. Here is an example.

John's report card has arrived, and it appears that his grades are slipping. His parents are concerned. They have a talk with him about it.

"John, your grades are dropping. What's wrong?

Are you not paying attention in class? You know if you do not make top grades you will not get into a good college. What do you have to say for yourself?"

This comment went straight to the problem, then to an assumed cause, then to a undesired result putting John in a position of assumed guilt. John's Self-Image is being hammered. Every time you think about something, it creates an imprint in your Self-Image. John is picturing that his grades are dropping. His Self-Image is imprinting that it is like him to make this happen. Next, he imagines that his parents think he is not paying attention in class. Whether this is true or not, the picture still creates an imprint, and the chance that this will become a pattern in the future is improved. These Imprints did not have to happen.

So, with Self-Image in mind, let's see if we can have a better conversation with John concerning his grades.

"John, we would like to see your grades return to the top. What do you think you need to do to get them there this semester? Give John a chance to talk about what he needs to do, and then make some suggestions of your own if needed. Again, I am not saying you never address the problem. One time when you must speak of a problem is if John does not realize he has one or is not informed about the possible adverse results of individual actions. I'm suggesting you minor in talking about the problem and major in talking about the solutions.

My mother's way of influencing the man I was becoming was through praise. She understood that the world would praise me for accomplishment, but it was her job to praise me for becoming. Here is an example.

"You know what I like about you son is you are a man of your word. We can always count on you, to tell the truth."

Always look for ways to praise who your children are and how they do things and not just the results. Praising this way is a powerful way to build who they are becoming.

Chapter 6
Goal Getting

Winners have one thing in common. They are goal getters. Ask parents if it is important for their kids to have goals and most will say it is important.

What do you think? What is a goal? What is the difference between having a goal and setting a goal? Is there a system for setting goals that dramatically improves the probability of attaining them? What is the difference between goal setting and goal getting? Who is responsible for making sure your young performers know the answers to these questions?

A simple definition of a goal is something you want to do, have, or be. A wish is something you define with no plan to get it, and you do not change your behavior even a little bit to do anything about moving toward it. A goal has a specific finish line. It is defined so well that if someone asks you if you have a goal you do not hesitate to say so. For it to meet our definition of a goal, it should include the date something is due, ends or expires.

Goal setting is something that almost everyone thinks is important but for some reason, we cannot remember anyone teaching us how to do it. Did you learn how to set goals in grade school? Did you take a course in goal setting in college? Were you taught it in church or synagogue? Did your mother or father or someone in your family set you down and show you a goal setting system? If so, congratulations, you are in the minority.

If you are like me, no one taught you how to set goals as a young person. Chances are, if you do not show your young performers how to set goals properly, they will struggle unnecessarily for the rest of their life to attain them.

Goal Setting Methods to Avoid

Goal Setting is a common practice among the winners. We are going to look at Goal Setting in this chapter, why it works for some and is ineffective for others. Then, I will give you a Goal Setting system that works.

Goal Setting is not easy for many people to do and here is why. First, there are two common methods of setting goals that most people try and neither of them work well; Reasonable Goal Setting and Big-Sky.

Some people believe you should always attain

your goals, so they try to set reasonable ones. They will look at what they did last period and move up the scoring a bit, and that will be their expectation for the next time. Sound right? I don't know a single Olympic Gold Medalist that used this method successfully. Why? There is nothing reasonable about winning a Gold Medal in the Olympics or setting a world record or reaching a dominant status in your sport. Big goals are more irrational than realistic. If you want to be realistic, you had better keep your goals low. Do that, and you will be beaten so often you will soon begin to doubt the system and abandon it. I see this happen all too often. Another variant of this scheme is to be vague in defining your goal. "I want to do better this year!" Really? What does BETTER mean?

Now, let's let's move on to the other system. I call it Big-Sky. The advantage of this method is that there are no upper limits to the goals. "My goal is to win every competition this year, breaking all of the records and beating everyone." You've got to admit this sounds appealing. Who wouldn't want to have a year like that? If you try this system, you are almost guaranteed to miss your goal. Most people who have banner years rarely, if ever, anticipate it would happen just that way. The BEST years of the BEST players are rarely foreseen in advance. Why? I believe it is because the elite are not thinking about the outcome. They are thinking about execution.

Both of these flawed goal setting systems are

outcome oriented, and that is the big problem. The focus is on the score or winning the competition. It should be in the process of getting a score that can win the game. You must tell your young performers once they take their mind off of score and focus on the process of performing well, they are dealing with something they alone can control. They cannot control what it will take to win a competition. They cannot control what other competitors do, and often you cannot even predict with accuracy what score will win a contest. But they can define a process. The process is what they can control and only what they can control. A process can be defined, and anything that can be defined can be duplicated.

Here is what I tell my students.

"You can predict and control how many days a week you train. You can monitor the discipline of your efforts. You can control what you choose to think about and do. You can determine the competitions you enter and how you decide to train for them. Only set goals on things that YOU can control. Keep your focus on you, not your competitors. Rehearse in your mind the process of executing a combination of mental feelings and technical moves that get results. Your success is determined by how well you can control what is in front of you, not by worrying about the outcome."

Most books on goal setting are result oriented, and I have a problem with that. I have no problem with setting a goal to have a winning performance, move up in a class or to make the team, if you are setting the goal to identify the process of attaining the goal. Remember attainment and accomplishment are not the same things. Accomplishment is all about the outcome, and it is important. We determine who wins by accomplishment. It is the score, the color of medal and the place on the list of competitors at the scoreboard. What it does not measure is what your young performers learned or their growth as a competitor. It does not measure who they have BE-COME. Attainment is the total of accomplishment and becoming.

Winning is more than just a way to measure the outcome. It also reflects who the person has become. It is a mirror to life; a snapshot of who this player is as well as how high he can score. We compete on the field as we compete in life. We become competitors. Attainment, consisting of becoming something, should be our goal, not the accomplishment alone.

Teach your children to goal set for both what they want to accomplish AND who they wish to become in the process.

You may need to help them to look at more than the outcome, and to determine the things they need to change about themselves to reach their goals. Assist them to develop the attitudes they need to succeed and not just the skills. Winning is the total package. It is control over both the mental and physical processes. We become skilled. We become confident.

We become champions.

Setting goals will help them plan, and that's beneficial, but there are dangers to avoid as well. One mistake many young people make is to equate their worth as a person with whether they reach their goals or not. If I reach the target, I am successful, but if I miss it, I'm a failure. If I make an A, I am an outstanding person. If I get a C, I'm average, and a failure if I get an F. The truth is their value as a person is more a function of their character, their beliefs, and their actions towards others, than the results on the playing field or a grade on a test.

Three Stages to Every Goal

There are three stages to every goal. The first two are well known by everyone. The third stage is one of the items of importance that only the top 5% seem to know. It is vital you understand and can teach the all three stages to your children.

The first stage I'm going to call Attraction. The focus is on the benefits of obtaining the goal. We only see the advantages, ignoring the disadvantages.

When I was in my 50's, I set a goal to learn more about Information Technology. I discovered DeVry University had a program that would allow a person with a bachelor's degree to obtain a BS in Information Technology in one year if they were willing to go to class on Friday and Saturday for 12 months. The cost seemed reasonable, and I could still work at my vocation. I started thinking about what this goal could do for me. I knew I needed more than a basic computer understanding to move my company into the Internet age. I felt this would give me the skills to significantly improve the way Mental Management was presented and improve our financial options. I registered for school and began classes determined to make straight A's. I was in Attraction.

Second Stage

When we set goals, we are not always able to foresee all of the obstacles in the way of achieving them. I hit stage two, I call Distraction, in my first exam in C programming. I'd studied well for the exam and felt prepared. The first question was worth 25% of my grade and I was clueless as to how to form an answer. With no chance at an A, I began to think about all of the things I did not like about going to school. I had to spend my weekends in class. That very test day I was being inducted into the Hall of Fame at the Army Marksmanship Unit in Ft. Benning Georgia and I could not be there to accept my award because of this dumb class. Maybe this was a bad idea. Who cares if I have another degree? Studying is taking up way too much time for the results I am getting. I cannot even answer the first question. Distraction is when you stop thinking about the benefits and only think about the costs.

Third Stage

If you stay in this stage, there is a strong possibility that you will fail to reach your goal. You must move on to the next stage called Traction. Traction is where you stop thinking about the benefits or the costs and think only about what you have to change about you to make it work. You do not stop working on the goal, but you start working on your attitude. I had to change my attitude about this test. I skipped the first question, answered the remaining ones and turned in my paper to the professor saying, "That's the best 75 you will ever see!" He looked at my paper, noticing I'd not even attempted to answer the first question and remarked, "Oh, I teach both Cobol and C. That's a Cobol question I used by mistake. I will have to throw that one out." I got my A and graduated with a 4.0.

Teach your children, at times when all seems lost when they are ready to throw in the towel; success may be just around the corner if they move to the Traction stage of the goal.

Chapter 7

Mental Management® Goal Setting System

If your son or daughter sets a goal to graduate from a university, you can obtain a list of the courses they need to accomplish a degree. A course catalog will tell you all you need to know to achieve the goal. This is called a Replicable Goal. All Replicable Goals have a recipe. Everything you need do it is known in advance. No surprises. If you accomplish the required tasks, you are guaranteed to reach the goal.

If, however, your child has as a goal to win a gymnastics competition or become valedictorian of her school this is another matter entirely. This is called a Unique Goal, and no recipe will guarantee success. Only one person can achieve this goal. Every person that has won in the past has taken a unique path to winning. Improving the probability of attainment is the most you can hope for in this case.

There is a process I have learned from my Olympic training experience you can use to help your young performers set both their Replicable and Unique goals. I suggest that you prepare them to only use this system with goals that are exciting, are out of reach but not out of sight and that will require significant time and change of behavior to attain.

Mental Management® Goal Setting System.

Step Number 1

"Determine a dream worth trading your life for."

My grandfather was a mail carrier in the central Texas town of Comanche. As a young teen, I loved to help him deliver the mail out in the country because he would let me drive. Grandad taught all his grandkids to drive a car. He did not seem to mind if we ran over things and his old Ford sedan had the dings to prove it. He made us feel grown up, and there was always a Dr. Pepper and a bag of peanuts as a treat at the end of the route. When I was in my first year of college, he had a heart attack while visiting us. It was something he was not able to overcome. At the hospital, we were all allowed some private time with him, and I knew it was probably the last time I would be with him. As I sat down next to his bed, he gave me some sound advice that has been with me all my life.

"Lanny, as I face the end, I regret that I've never done anything in my life a typical person couldn't have done. I always made the safe choice, never taking a risk. I've never been out of the state of Texas. I've never competed in anything, joined anything or built anything. I've done a good job of dodging the perils of life, but in the process, I missed a part of living. Don't let caution keep you from experiencing life. Go out and find a dream worth trading your life for because, in the end, that is what you are doing. Set big goals. You do not want to end up regretting your life." That was the last thing my grandfather said to me.

Particular care is needed in this step to ensure the goal is something that only they can control. Goal setting to win a competition does not qualify because your kids cannot control what other people do. I suggest my client's goal set for a tournament winning performance instead.

Help them to make the goal specific. It is important for your children to know what it means to cross the finish line. Ask them to visualize what it would feel like to reach the end.

Who do they need to become and what do they need to accomplish for the goal to be met?

It is vital that your children understand at the outset that reaching a goal is only part of the process. Who they became in the process is in many ways more important. They should be proud of not only what they have done, but also the way in which they did it.

Step Number 2

Decide when you want it.

Putting a time limit on goals helps to formulate a plan to achieve them. If a goal was to save $1,000 in 1,000 days, you could do that by putting a dollar a day in the bank. If the time limit advanced to $1,000 in one month, the plan would have to change.

Step Number 3

List the pay-value.

Ask, why do you want the goal? List all the reasons that are important to you for achieving the goal. Make certain the goal they set is big enough to be life-changing for them. Many things motivate people, but these three are the most useful to parents: the promise of gain, fear of loss, and recognition. Help them set a goal big enough to move them to change habits or attitudes. If the goal is too small, they will not appreciate it when accomplished..

The goal must be something they want, not what you want for them.

Is the pay-value personally rewarding to them? I had a friend in college, a pre-dentistry major, who did not want to be a dentist. His grandfather and father were dentists, and the family expected him to join the profession. He hated school as a result.

When my twin sons, Brian and Troy, were in

their early teens I owned and operated the International Shooting School. I think most parents want their kids to walk in their footsteps. My father was a Major in the US Army, loved horses and played guitar. I was a Major in the Army, loved horses and played guitar. But, I was concerned. I did not want to push my sons into rifle shooting, remembering my friend in college. Fortunately for me, they were outstanding soccer players. I assumed their sport would be soccer not shooting, but they kept bugging me to let them shoot. Soon they were accomplished in both sports, winning competitions in rifle, and qualifying for Team USA to play an international soccer tour in Europe. With college scholarships available in both sports it soon became evident they would have to make a choice between them. I did my best to stay out of the decision. Although both play soccer to this day, they chose the rifle and obtained full-ride scholarships at the University of Texas at El Paso.

Step Number 4

Honestly evaluate the obstacles in your way.

One way to determine the obstacles is to ask your young performer "Why don't you have the goal now?" What do they need to learn? Are new skills needed? What equipment, coaching opportunities or competitive experience are required? Perhaps the area you can be of the most help in the goal-setting process is in making them aware of challenges ahead. Their future is populated with both obstacles and opportunities. The chances are good that you have been where they are heading. Parents must walk a fine line here. Learning to overcome obstacles is essential for growth. If the tasks before your young performers are too high, they might become so discouraged that their Self-Image suffers irreparable damage. If however, the way is too easy, they do not grow strong enough to handle the perils of life ahead.

It is human nature to desire to economize effort, time and money. Young people tend to underestimate the importance of obstacles when they do this. Have you heard this before?

"Without resistance an exercise produces no muscle."

"You tend to get out of something what you put into it."

"Rules are there for a reason."

"People appreciate things in direct proportion to the price they pay for them."

What habits and attitudes must they master to acquire the goal? Remember, nothing is going to get better until they get better. They must change. What new skills do they need? How are they going to acquire them?

You almost always have to give up something good to make room for something great!

Step Number 5

What is your plan to get your goal?

The difference between a wish and a goal is that a goal has a written plan to get it. Wishes usually do not come true. Goals, with written plans, have a much better chance of being reached. In Step Number 4, several reasons were discovered why the goal is presently unattainable. Help them prepare a written plan to overcome each obstacle. Now, the price they must pay for the goal becomes clearer. Planning saves time and provides direction. Do not be surprised if they cannot always see the obstacles in their way.

Tell them, "Life has a way of adding challenges once you are on your way. Remember you cannot always see all of the opportunities at the start. Doors have a way of opening for you if you look for them."

Step Number 6

Evaluate your plan before you proceed.

Ask them some questions.

"How will going for this goal affect the other priorities in my life?"

"How will the people I care about be affected by this plan?"

"Is the plan consistent with my fundamental values?"

"Do I believe my plan will work?"

"Do I believe I can work the plan?"

"Is the prize worth the price?"

This is one of the most important steps in the goal-setting process. If they are comfortable with their answers to these questions, chances are their goal and plan are acceptable. If the scheme and pay-value do not match, or they are not comfortable with any answer, something needs to change. Maybe they need to modify the goal, the time limit, the plan or all three.

Step Number 7

Schedule your plan.

When my daughter was very young, she overheard me saying, "If it is on the calendar it will get done." The next day I saw marked on my calendar in crayon, "Buy Heather a stuffed animal." What do you think I did?

Step 7 is a major turning point. Scheduling adds a commitment to the planning process. There is a huge difference between a person saying they are going to do something and blocking out a time to do it on a calendar. If a goal is not scheduled, it will likely not get done. Scheduling is much more than just hanging up a calendar to easily see the day of the week. I am suggesting you teach them to log what they are going to do, and when. Something magic happens when a child selects a date and writes in a task to be completed. Doing the work becomes an integrity issue. Recording a task is a promise to do it by that date. Being a person that can be relied upon to fulfill their promise is a fundamental value of all winners. It is worthy of your time to teach it. Both a large monthly calendar on the wall and a calendar app on the tablet and phone are essential in today's world. If you fail to instruct your children early on the importance of scheduling their time, it may be years before they benefit from this tool. I believe until goals are up on a calendar the commitment to their attainment is questionable.

Step Number 8

Start Now.

Tell your young winners.

"You are now ready to go. Begin right away. Do not hesitate."

"Things will get not better if you wait to get started?"

"Clear the deck of time wasters and execute the first step of your plan right now."

"Put out high-quality effort, consistently over time, and you can do anything you dream of doing."

Step Number 9

Before reaching your goal always set a new

one to take its place.

The day I received my Olympic gold medal was both fulfilling and traumatic for me. The award ceremony was great. Hearing my country's national anthem being played while the flag was raised high in front of me was the best of feelings. However, later that day, I had an unexpected experience. I suffered severe depression, and I didn't know why. My wife recognized the problem and helped me understand that I had reached my goal. I had not goal-set beyond the Olympic Games, and for the first time in 20 years, I was without direction. Once I set a new goal, I was again at peace.

Step Number 10

Hold on to the end or trade up.

Early in my career, I set a goal to win the national title in the air rifle event. I thought that it would take a 380 out of 400 to win. In the match, I was down 19 points with three shots left to go. I shot a nine. Now I figured, I had to shoot two tens, to win. Shooting another nine, I was down below 380. I rationalized that I could not win, so I mentally gave up. I quickly put up the rifle and shot an eight. I finished with a 377. That year the national championship went for a 378. Had I been persistent, I would have won the title. Stay with your plan until it is finished. By the way, counting my score while shooting was the mental error that got me into trouble in this example.

Your children will always want to reach their goals, and that is a good thing, but there is one time when reaching their goal is not optimum. Do not be surprised if, on their way to one goal they discover another, that means more to them than the one they are working to achieve. This is called trading up.

Tell them, "If you trade up to the new goal you should view the first goal as having completed its purpose. Finding a new target that means more to you than the first one is very rewarding, but be cautious not to trade your current one for one that is easier to reach. If you do, you may regret the choice."

Young performers are often interested in many things, setting goals in all of them soon exhausts their time and resources available. Prioritizing is the key here. Making a list of everything they would like to do is a good start. Then choose the one that is most important and schedule it. If more time is remaining, they can add an additional one.

Chapter 8

What Every Parent Should Know

A comment I hear most from my students is "I wish I'd known this information sooner." In this chapter, we will look at seven concepts that will give you an advantage in working with your children as they begin to compete. Many of the top Olympic and professional coaches in the world use these concepts. There is no reason why you cannot use them as well.

1. Understanding the Three Participation Levels

There are three participation levels in any competitive activity, Training to Learn, Training to Compete, and Training to Excel. It is vital that you determine which participation level your young performer is currently in to work properly with them. The levels provide you with guidance on what to expect from your child and what they should expect from you.

Training to Learn

Everyone begins in the Training to Learn participation level. Examples are playing sandlot baseball or softball with schoolmates, playing recreational tennis with friends, checking out the archery club, participating in a pickup game at the basketball court, or organizing a soccer or flag football game.

In this level, the athlete is "interested." So, the parent should be "interested." Remember when you were young? How many activities did you try out? There are no organized competitions at this level. It is the place to evaluate activities, perhaps finding one that might be worthy of moving to the Training to Compete level. Your job is to aid your children to discover what turns them on. What do they like to do? Help them gather details about the sport. Go to the library for books. Search the Internet for information. The focus is on enjoyment and discovery of interest.

Your focus in Training to Learn is to gather information, encourage them, and make opportunities available. You are not spending money on lessons or expensive equipment at this stage because they are not going to competitions. Be careful not to get ahead of your child. Look for signs they want to get serious or have a desire to compete. When this happens, you are both ready for the next level.

Training to Compete

Training to Compete is a significant progression from "interested" to "committed." Examples of this level are any sport or activity that competes for awards or recognition such as organized athletics that have a season, league soccer, competitive band, cheer, debate team, competitive choir, or a pursuit that rewards a letter in school.

The transition begins with the first competition. Kids may be enthusiastic in the Training to Learn level but as they enter formal competition the demands for a greater need of involvement from both of you increases. When you sign up your young performer for a competitive activity, you become their primary source of support. You provide funds, transportation, and become the president of their booster club. A significant investment of your time, energy, and money is required. Ideally, there should be a balanced commitment from both you and your kids.

People, including kids, appreciate things in direct proportion to the price they pay for them.

If kids are respectful, appreciative, hard-working and dedicated to the activity, but the parents show little commitment to providing interest and support, this may become a problem. The reverse is also true. If parents provide adequate resources and support but notice little commitment, effort or appreciation from the beneficiary, some correction toward a balance is needed. Keeping this balance is one of the most difficult things for most families to do well. Situations are not always ideal. Sometimes, funds are just not available for everything, mom or dad cannot be at every performance, and disappointment is often inevitable. Kids are not perfect, having good and bad days vacillating between devotion and disdain. This attitude can misrepresent them as not caring when they are just struggling through adolescence.

My major point in the Training to Compete level is both the parent and the child need to be "committed equally" to the activity as best possible, and flexible at times. An "interested" parent and a "committed" child will not work any better than a "committed" parent and an "interested" child.

Training to Excel

I can remember when Earl Woods brought his two-year-old son Tiger on the Mike Douglas Show with Bob Hope. Tiger was a cute kid, but that is not why everyone was amazed; Tiger could hit a decent shot at two. Mike Douglas began to question Earl Woods.

"How many hours do you make him practice?"

"Make him practice? I can't get him off of the course," replied Earl.

Tiger won his first golf tournament at age eight, and 79 tournaments on the PGA Tour so far. He and his father Earl are examples of Training to Excel.

Performers in this level are beyond "interested" or "committed." They have an intense desire and enthusiasm for the activity. They are "passionate." Malcolm Gladwell in his book *Outliers* talks about the Ten Thousand Hour Rule. If you want to become good at something, you need to train approximately 5,000 hours, but to become great, you will need 10,000. In my experience, there is only one way a person will invest 10,000 hours willingly in anything. It requires passion.

In both high school and college, I went to school early every day to shoot. I was on the rifle team. After class, most days you would find me on the range again. Most of my teammates shot twice a week. They were in the Training to Compete level, and practice was something they "had" to do. I shot twice a day. I was in the Training to Excel level, and practice was something I "got" to do. I was the only four-year collegiate All-American in my university shooting team, and as far as I know, none of my team continued to compete after college.

Please understand, I am not a better person, more dedicated, or superior in any way to my teammates. The fact that, for some unknown reason, I was blessed with a higher level of passion is the only difference. I had no choice in the matter. I did not ask to have a passion for shooting any more than Tiger Woods did for golf. I do not believe you can teach passion at the level the dominate players in the world possess it. Passion seems to be temporary for some and more permanent for others. I do not completely understand it, but I know what it feels like to have it, and it is uncommon.

Defining the Training to Excel level?

How do you determine if your children have passion? First, passion is rare. The vast majority of competitors are in the Training to Compete level. Training to Compete is an honorable place and passion is not necessary for a good performance. But, when your children are willing to sacrifice their own time and money, when practicing the activity is more important than being with their friends, and they seem to talk non-stop about nothing else; they have passion.

Someone at Training to Compete will focus on what the people in the middle of the leaderboard are doing. When your child begins to focus exclusively on what the winners are doing, get ready; they are moving into the Training to Excel level. A word of caution is required here. Sometimes performers, and parents, have a desire to excel without being willing to pay the price. Having Training to Excel goals with Training to Compete investment is a prescription for failure for both the child and the parent.

You should do everything in your power to match your involvement to your young performer's participation level if possible. I have seen situations where parents are in Training to Excel, and the child is still in Training to Compete. The parent is the one who is "passionate," while the child is "committed." Parents who live vicariously through their children are often in this group. What parent would not want their child to excel? "My kid is the star quarterback." "My daughter is the valedictorian." What if your child is not ready for your level of expectation? Do you see the kind of pressure you put on them when you are out of sync with their participation level?

Here is an example of why I am concerned. Several years ago, I provided mental training to a promising young athlete. Her mother told me, "I want my daughter to dominate. I've bought her the best equipment and taken her to the best coaches. I've sacrificed a lot of time and money on her. She just doesn't seem to want to work hard enough to win." This statement is problematic. I felt her daughter was working just fine for an athlete in the Training to Compete level. Then she said, "I told her if she doesn't start winning and get a college scholarship, she will be letting me down." Mom is in Training to Excel, and her daughter is in Training to Compete. Putting a guilt trip on her daughter will not get her to win, it will get her to resent Mom.

A "committed" player will have trouble competing against a "passionate" one. Passionate performers are exceedingly rare among the population but are common among the top 5% that does 95% of the winning. If your child ranks in the top ten in any subject or sport in their school, I'm betting they are in Training to Excel.

Please do not miss the point I am making. If your young performers are "interested," be "interested," if "committed," you should be as well. But, if they are "passionate;" support them with everything you've got; you may have the best who has ever played this sport in your family.

2. The Four Stages of Learning

The Dependent Stage

Tim Keller says in his book *Reason for God.*

Children come into the world in a condition of complete dependence. They cannot operate as self-sufficient, independent agents unless their parents give up much of their own independence and freedom for years. If you don't allow your children to hinder your freedom in work and play at all, and if you only get to your children when it doesn't inconvenience you, your children will grow up physically only. In all sorts of other ways, they will remain emotionally needy, troubled, and overdependent. The choice is clear. You can either sacrifice your freedom or theirs. It's them or you. To love your children well, you must decrease that they may increase.

When your children are very young, and totally sustained by you, they are in the Dependent Stage of Learning. Mom and Dad make the decisions, and life is programmed to a large extent for them. The Principle of External Influence defines this stage. It says, people will do far more, with greater efficiency, if told what to do by others instead of deciding for themselves.

I believe the Dependent Stage serves a great purpose in developing young performers because the best way to learn something quickly is to go sit at the feet of the master and say "Teach me." The student does not have to determine the correct thing to do; it is decided for them.

Marine Corps Boot Camp is a good example. The Drill Instructor does not ask the recruit what he would like to do today; he tells him. Few people would do what recruits are asked to do on their own. If you engage a fitness instructor, you will tend to work harder and longer in a gym session. Children in the Dependent Stage should often hear "This is what you need to do." from the parent. Increased efficiency is an advantage of this stage, but it comes at the cost of loss of freedom to choose. If you leave your children in the Dependent Stage throughout their school years, always deciding for them, they will likely be still living with you at 35.

The Inter-Dependent Stage

In the Inter-Dependent Stage, a choice is encouraged. The Power of Self-Direction states that people will do things with greater enthusiasm, and energy if it is their idea. We encourage our teens to make decisions for themselves while setting boundaries to protect them from harm. In the Inter-Dependent Stage, you work together with your young person. Hopefully, many decisions are made by them with you observing, instead of deciding. This stage demands high self-direction and limited external influence.

An appropriate thing to say in the Inter-Dependent Stage is "What do you think you should do?" You should transition from telling your child what to do to asking them what they think they should do – and hoping that they will come up with the right answer.

The Co-Dependent Stage

As your kids begin to interact with others, they will be in the Co-Dependent Stage of Learning much of the time; learning from and being influenced by peers. Their Self-Image is shaped, in part, by the statements and actions of the players they are around. As your young performers grow, your influence in their lives gradually drops as they become increasingly affected by others. By the time, they start college; you are history. Your job at this stage is to pay attention to the statements, attitudes, and habits of the athletes and friends your kids choose.

The Independent Stage

I have children who are married. I do not offer advice on anything until asked. They are heads of their families and are no longer dependent on my wife and me. Occasionally, a request is made to seek advice. Making us feel special when it happens, thinking we might still know something they do not know. But, they no longer need us. There will come a day when your children will cease to require you as their coach. When this happens, you have entered the Independent Stage of Learning. As parents, we need to be ready to hand over our most precious people to the care of someone else, no matter how much it pains us. That is your job in the Independent Stage. It sounds easy, but it's not.

Your young performers will advance through these stages many times in their life. I hope this information may give you an edge in helping them. I will have more to say about the stages of learning in a later chapter on dealing with coaches.

There are connections between the three Participation Levels and the Four Stages of Learning. Athletes in the Training to Learn level tend to be in the Dependent stage. Those in the Training to Compete are most likely in the Inter-Dependent, while the Training to Excel favors the Independent stage. Interestingly, the Co-Dependent plays heavily in all three stages. The better players you are around, the better you play.

3. Using Readiness Factors

Once you have determined the Participation Level and Stage of Learning of your young performer, you are ready to use readiness factors to accelerate your effectiveness as a parent mental coach. I hope that you'll agree with me that successful people are willing and able to do what unsuccessful people are not willing or not able to do. So, let's break down readiness factors along those lines. There are four Readiness Factors.

R1 (Readiness Factor #1) – is someone that's

neither willing nor able to do a task. This person doesn't know that something is important, and does not know how to do it. We have an excellent example of this in Mental Management. We've developed a performance journal for athletes called Performance Analysis, which we feel is critical to building Self-Image. (We will have a lot to say about journals in the next chapter.) Most of our students have no prior experience in using a performance journal. They do not know it is an important thing for them to do, and they have no training in how to use it. R1s need to be told "what" to do.

Let's look at an R2. An R2 is someone who is willing, but not able. This person says "OK, I understand that your performance journal is a good thing to do, but I don't know how to do it." So, they are asking you to "teach" them. With an R1, you're telling them what to do, whereas, with an R2, you're showing them "how" to do it.

The R3 is someone who is able, but not willing. This person knows how to do the task, but for some reason, fails to do it. Our R3, while knowing how to keep a journal, has lost the motivation to keep it. They need to be reminded "why" it is important to continue. So, an R3 need to be motivated.

An R4 is someone who is both willing and able. This person knows what to do and does it. You must remember to tell your R4, "Good Job!" I think far too many parents scold their kids when they fail to perform and forget to praise them when they remember. Some Moms and Dads tend to ignore kids behaving in a proper manner. They need to be told, "I appreciate the good behavior." The squeaky wheel often gets the attention. Performers need to be recognized when they are doing things well. R4s need confirmation.

4. Applying the Appropriate Coaching Process

Once you determine a person's readiness factor, you can match that up to a coaching process. There are four Coaching Processes.

Informing - telling people what to do.

Teaching – telling people how.

Motivating – telling people why.

Confirming – praising those that do it.

Now, why is all this important? Your kids are always in one of the four Readiness Factors concerning an element in their performance activity. Each Coaching Process is best used with an appropriate Readiness Factor.

R1 requires Informing - What

R2 needs Teaching - How

R3 demands Motivation - Why

R4 requires Confirming - Are

The Readiness Factor determines the Coaching Process, and how you should talk to your kids. Here is an example. Taking out the trash is a chore assigned to Bobby by his parents. His mom notices that the trash is full and Bobby is ignoring it. He is not an R1. Bobby is well informed about his duties. He is not an R2. He knows how to take out the trash. He is an R3. Bobby needs some motivation and hears mom say. "Bobby, you cannot have dad's car for your date tonight if you do not finish all of your chores. Understand?" Bobby is now motivated.

Here is my point. Using any other Coaching Process would be inappropriate. Let's look at another example. Bobby's dad confronts him.

"You need to do your homework," says Dad.

"I don't understand my assignment."

"Just get it done!"

Dad is acting like Bobby is an R1, telling him what he needs to do instead of how to do it. Bobby is an R2. He needs teaching. Bobby needs to hear his dad say "Let's look at the assignment together. I'll be happy to help you if I can."

The process is simple.

First, determine the task - Bobby 's homework.

Second, determine the Readiness Factor - R2. Bobby needs to be taught.

Finally, determine the appropriate Coaching Process. Bobby does not need to be informed, motivated or confirmed. No other process will work. Dad needs to teach.

What if parents only tell their children what they need to do, seeming stuck in the Informing process? Their kids are rarely taught, motivated or praised. Do you see the problem?

My hope is you will be sensitive to your children's Readiness Factors when talking to them. Remember to Inform when they need to know something is important, to Teach when they need to know how to do a task, to Motivate when needing a push, and most importantly, to Praise them when they succeed.

5. Proactive vs. Reactive

Most sports or performances can be divided into either Proactive or Reactive mode as they relate to mental skills. Sports like shooting, archery, and golf are Proactive; the performer has control over the start of the action. The action is mostly a duplication of a previously practiced move. You have time to execute a defined Mental Process on each shot.

The Mental Process is what you think about before, during, and after a task. Some sports, primarily Proactive in nature, such as rifle shooting and golf allow you to define both your Shot Routine and your Mental Process. The Shot Routine is what you are physically doing while the Mental Process is what you are thinking about while you are doing it. In Proactive applications, you have time to think about your target, your strategy and the best way to attack the situation, possibly changing the shot you choose to attempt.

Some sports such as Basketball, Football and Tennis are both Proactive and Reactive depending on the situation. Shooting a free-throw or kicking a field goal are Proactive in nature. All of the action while the ball is in play is Reactive. The player does not have time to plan ahead. Elite players tell us that to execute a play correctly or to respond effectively to an opponent while the ball is in play, you must move by a conditioned process rather than a conscious one. By the time the conscious mind has formulated a plan, the time for action has passed, and the opponent has the advantage. The action must be Reactive, and speed is the key. In Reactive sports, the subconscious must be conditioned through training to respond to recurrent situations without waiting for the conscious process to make a decision.

If your kids are in a Proactive sport, they have time to run a Mental Process, but if the sport is more Reactive, they must rely on training drills to condition the subconscious to react, as there is not enough time for the conscious mind to respond to the task. A player can run a Mental Process on a serve in tennis but must rely on their conditioned instincts to win the point once the ball is in play.

6. Understanding Praise and Criticism

Both Praise and Criticism are forms of imprinting. The Self-Image is the repository of all of the imprints received since birth, both positive and negative, controlling the decisions your children make, determining what they accomplish and who they become.

Praise comes in two forms. We tend to recognize the results of a task well done while admiring the internal attributes of the one performing it. Both are important for different reasons. Praise results; you reward Accomplishment. Praise the way the child behaved while obtaining the results; you reward Becoming. If you believe who your kids become is more important than what they accomplish you must praise who they are more often than what they do. I'm suggesting you go out of your way to notice when they exhibit behavior that shows integrity. Here are some examples:

"John, one thing I like about you is you are a man of your word. I can always count on your truthfulness."

"Jane, you are a helpful person, always willing to lend a hand without being asked."

"You always seem to be in a good mood. I appreciate that about you."

"You always seem to be courteous to others, well mannered and considerate."

"You always seem to have something good to say about your friends. You do not complain. That attitude will take you far in the future."

Additionally, you should encourage your kids to credit themselves with good behavior and not just the desired results. Your young performer's Self-Image needs two nutrients to grow; praise from others and praise from self. The world will reward Accomplishment to a degree but rarely recognize Becoming. Your job as a parent/coach is to honor good habits and attitudes while encouraging your children to do the same.

Criticism is the opposite of Praise, but like it in one respect; it also comes in two forms. Form One, we tend to condemn poor results. There is a big difference between criticizing and correcting. There is no condemnation intended in a correction. To criticize one's results carries an expression of disfavor. The second form of criticism is far more destructive when we condemn who they are. Telling someone, they are a loser hurts more than criticizing a single failed attempt. Criticizing who they are, attacks their Self-Image. "Sticks and stones may break my bones, but words will never hurt me," is wrong. Words may not break bones, but most of us can remember times in our past where words of criticism destroyed us. Words that condemn from a family member cut deep. Correcting is a parent/coaches job. When we do it lovingly, there is never a chance for it becoming criticism.

I find "beating themselves up" is a common problem with my adult clients. I often ask, "How is that working out for you?" They always say "Not well." This bad habit is Self-Criticism and is devastating to the Self-Image. I believe Self-Criticism starts at an early age. Young children sometimes use demeaning language toward themselves. "I'm just not good at math." Where do you suppose they got the idea to use such words? I choose to blame their environment. When children hear others say such things, they tend to copy them. Here is my point. When you find your kids beating themselves up, you must correct this abusive behavior. Remind them that if they prepare properly, there are few things in life they cannot accomplish.

Mom's often say, "If you do not have something good to say about someone, do not say anything at all!" She was right. I have just one regret in my life. I wish I could take back everything hurtful I said about anyone because I cannot think of a time when it ever helped me. That also applies to what you say about yourself. Correction is OK; Criticism is not!

7. The Three Steps to Consistency

Why is McDonald's the largest restaurant chain in the world? They do not make the best hamburgers; you do, but if you order a Big Mac in Boston, it will taste like the one you ordered in Baja. Consistency is the achievement of a level of performance that does not vary greatly in quality over time.

If your children compete, they are likely engaged in either a Sport of Constants or a Sport of Variables. Archery, like rifle shooting, is a Sport of Constants; the only variable is the wind. In indoor archery, there are no variables at all. In a Sport of Constants, introducing a variable, like changing your length of draw, creates lost points. The top performers work diligently to execute both what they physically do and what they think about, in the same way, every time. Consistency is critical in a Sport of Constants.

Golf is a Sport of Variables. Everything changes in this game. The courses vary; every target, distance, and shot are different from the previous one. Anything you make a constant in a Sport of Variables is an advantage. The top performers work diligently to execute both what they physically do and what they think about, in the same way, every time. Consistency is critical in a Sport of Variables.

Achieving consistency is not easy, and it is an ongoing challenge for your young performer throughout his/her career. We can, however, better understand a thing if we break it down into its elements. I offer three.

1. Carefully Choose Your Primary.

2. Master What You've Chosen.

3. Trust What You've Mastered.

Carefully Choose your Primary.

Your first step is to help your young performer define what they believe are the optimum things to think about and physically perform before, during and after the action phase of their sport. To achieve consistency, you must choose the very best way to execute a task. A golfer, for example, has at least three systems that impact the outcome of a golf shot. These are the technical system (how to move the club), the mental system (what to think about during the process) and the course management system (how to select the target, distance, club, and line). Elite players have determined a favored or primary way of performing each of these systems that tend to yield the best results. For example, a player should have a primary way of holding the club. The keys here are choosing a primary way and carefully defining it. You cannot grip the club the same way every time if you have not defined a primary way of holding it. How tightly do you hold it? How far from the end of the club do you place your hands? Where do you put your fingers on the club? There should be a primary order to each step in the process. The top 5% carfully choose their best way of doing everything.

What about your child's mental game? Do they have a defined mental game plan? Have they chosen their primary way to think before, during and after the action phase of their sport or application?

Elite performers have carefully defined ways of doing everything they do and think. I suggest that you have your kids take the time to write down what they have chosen as their best choice of thinking and executing. Carefully defining a primary will make the next step easier.

You Must Master What You Have Chosen.

Mastery is a relative term. It might mean different things to different people. The level of mastery I am referring to is to have enough understanding, control, and proficiency to be able to execute the process well enough to reach your goals with little conscious effort. To achieve this, you must stay with what you have chosen. You cannot be jumping around, experimenting with new things. You will never gain mastery if you do not train with a process long enough to master it. I have no way of knowing for certain how long it will take you to learn a skill, but I can give you some indicators that you are close to mastery.

You are getting close to mastery if you do not have to think about doing a skill to be able to do it well. In fact, if you have to think about a skill to perform, you are executing it consciously rather than subconsciously.

> *'Amateurs [musicians] practice until they can get it right; professionals practice until they can't get it wrong' (quoted by Harold Craxton, one-time professor at the Royal Academy of Music).*

When you cannot get it wrong, you are approaching mastery.

Here is another indicator. Once elite players master a task, they tend to stay with the method that yields success, preferring not to abandon it for something new. When your young performer, after they have attained a high level of skill, is no longer tempted to try a new way to do something, they are nearing mastery.

Beginners have a lot of doubt about their ability. Is this the correct way to perform or should I change? When you doubt, you are unable to trust. Young performers are especially vulnerable to trying something new that might be inferior to what they are using. Also, when you are having trouble, you tend to seek change. Now, do not get me wrong here, I realize as we learn, it is sometimes necessary to change our minds but can we at least agree that throwing out what you have brought with you to a competition and searching for something new while you are in the contest is a dangerous idea?

I suggest you encourage experimentation in training, not in competitions. Once your kids leave their last training session, agree to stay with what they have chosen. Remember, there are only two ways to get better; find something superior to what you are using and upgrade to it, or find something that works, and making it work more often. The top 5% that win 95% of the time tend to major in the latter method.

How long does it take to become great at something? Malcolm Gladwell in his book Outliers suggests the number is 10,000 hours. He says talent develops because of hours of quality practice. I would like to add that very time you change the primary you tend to restart the clock on the 10,000 hours.

You Must Trust What You Have Mastered.

Champions, who have paid the price to master a proven way to excel, do not need to worry about the possibility they might not perform well. All they need to do is duplicate what they have mastered.

Just trust it! Trust that all of those hours of training will be there when you need them. Remember, if it took you a long time to acquire a skill it will take you a long time to forget how to do it. Tell your kids to trust their training. Now, if you have spent little time in training, you may have little to trust. Remember, once you have mastered a skill, you can Over-Try but you cannot Over-Trust.

Consistency alone will not get you in the top 5%, but a lack of it will certainly keep you out.

Watching Your Kids Play

I've decided to share a story written a few years ago by my daughter, Heather Sumlin, about her daughter, Ashley, also known as "The Peas." We can learn a lot from our kids when we watch and listen. This article is reproduced exactly as it appeared in our Mentalcoach Newsletter. It is entitled "Mommy - Stop Cheering for Me!"

The Peas found a new passion: SOCCER. She loves to run and be outside; it's a great fit for her. Although secretly (not always so secretly) I want her to take up dance or pursue something with beauty, elegance and Air Conditioning, I'm learning to embrace soccer. Up until recently, the Peas had yet to score a goal. She would get the ball and then freeze or kick it and watch it roll. She wouldn't run after it with the aggression needed to be successful in this contact sport.

In her second to last game of the season, she tells me "Mommy don't cheer for me today. Please!"

"What? Why?" I said.

"When you cheer for me I lose my focus. I need to think about the ball, and when you cheer, I think about what you are saying and not what I am doing."

So I decided to play it her way and as much as I wanted to cheer and scream when she got the ball I kept my mouth shut tight. She scored two goals that game, her first two goals ever! She was aggressive, in the moment and fearless. She was a ball player, and for the first time, she was focused and triumphant in a game.

For the Peas, even though all the other parents are cheering, she hears me over all of them. Unknowingly, I was pulling her focus and keeping her from reaching her goal. I was coaching her from the sidelines, and that's not my job. She needs to pay attention to her real coach and her game plan, not me. I need to stand back and watch, enjoy, video tape maybe, but my cheering is not a helpful addition to the game, at least not for her. I'm thankful that she was mature enough at seven years old to realize that my cheering is a distraction to her and vocal enough to ask me to keep it down and let her focus.

I was a variable to her game and the only variable that she could change. Once my yelling was toned down, she was able to concentrate on the task at hand. Next season I may be the only parent without a sore throat after a game due to my silence, but I will listen to my daughter. I will be open to altering my parenting due to what her needs are, and I will do my best to allow the coaching to be done by the coach.

This experience made me wonder, why do we become so connected to what other people are doing and saying that we fail to keep our focus on what is right in front of us? It happens all of the time. We focus on things that will not help us to reach our goals.

Often we allow our environment to pull us from thinking about and acting on what we need to be doing. Unlike the 7-year-old Peas, we cannot change our situation in most cases. And over time Ashley will have to find a way to control her thoughts despite her environment as well. But what about the things we can control? What if we limited our distractions, focused on our tasks with confidence, clearly communicated what we need from others and checked all worry at the door. We too could be successful.

Chapter 9

The Performance Journal

A Performance Journal is a written record of what you have done, what you've learned and what you did right! Someone is likely coaching your children, and if they should ask them "How have you been doing?" It is probable they will say something like "OK, I guess." You can bet they cannot with precision remember what they've been doing because they have no record of it. I believe the primary reasons people do not keep a Performance Journal is they do not think it is important to do it and they do not know how to do it.

OK. Here is why your kids MUST record their progress in a Performance Journal. I'll give you four reasons.

First, they cannot manage what they do not measure. Simply put, your children cannot afford to be in the dark concerning their progress. Let's say they fall short of their goal in a competition. If they have a well-documented Performance Journal, they can quickly determine if their plan failed or they just failed to work their plan. Winning is not an accident. You must plan your work, work your plan and be accountable.

Secondly, I will not coach an individual without a Performance Journal. Why? Because by referring to the Performance Journal of my performers, I know how often they are practicing, how long the practice session lasts, what went on in the training session or competition, what worked and what did not work, the objective of the training, what was learned and accomplished. I know the exact equipment used when a change in equipment occurred and the reason for the modification. I know what the competition results were, what the weather was like on the field and the start time of the event. And what is even more important is if I can determine this level of information from the journal, then the performer can as well. How does anyone know this amount of detail if it is not recorded? If your young player is serious about beating their competition, they should not be willing to trust their memory on these critical issues. No journal? Getting better will take much longer. You can't manage what you don't measure.

Next, if you are using the journal only to record information you are not maximizing the utilization of a Performance Journal. I believe that the primary benefit of a Performance Journal is to build Self-Image by imprinting both real and rehearsed images. Every time we think about something it Imprints and shapes our Self-Image. I believe when we talk about something it Imprints with greater power than just thinking about it. Talking about a bad performance is a way to cause it to become a habit. We become what we think and say. Mental images that are written down have a greater impact on the Self-Image than those we only say. If you desire to change your Self-Image, make a habit of writing down what you wish to happen. You tend to become what you write. But, be careful, do not write about anything that you do not want to happen.

Finally, perhaps the best reason to keep a journal is your kid's competition is not going to do it. I am suggesting they invest five minutes a day in maintaining a journal to create the Self-Image of the Top 5%er. That is a bargain for the few that will go for it.

So, if having a Performance Journal is such a good idea why do so few people take the time to keep one. Again I'll give you my reasons.

First, they keep a diary, not a journal. My definition of a diary is to record your impressions, good and bad, of what happened today. Recording the statistics can be helpful, and we will do this as well in a Performance Journal, but if you record your mistakes you are making a huge mental error, and the Self-Image suffers. Let's say your child has a bad day at an event, and they record all of their mistakes. The Principle of Reinforcement works against them big time. They have just improved their chance of making these errors again in the future by writing them down

in the diary. A Performance Journal, by my definition, has no references to failure, bad experiences, or
poor performances. It is a Performance Journal not a
lack of Performance Journal. People who keep diaries often find their performance suffers in the future.
When this happens, they do the correct thing. They
throw the diary away. Diaries don't work, but Performance Journals do and are essential if you want to
maximize your performance in competitions.

Secondly, performers do not know how to keep
a Performance Journal and are rarely taught properly
by those who coach them. I recommend you teach
your kids to record critical information in a journal
every day at the end of training or competition. OK,
what should be in your children's Performance Journal?

They should have an equipment page that is
regularly updated every time they change anything.
They need a competition page to record scores in
competition and an easy way to relate them to the
journal pages. They should record this information
immediately after performing. People can remember
things only so long, so have them make journal entries before leaving the competition or training area
if possible.

Finally, most people will not keep a journal because they are just lazy. Look, if your children are
playing just to have fun this section may not be for
you, but if they want to win they must separate them-

selves from the competition. I understand they do not like to document things. They need to do it because not doing it is just not acceptable. It is not acceptable to be unable to remember what they have or have not done. It is not acceptable to make the same mistakes over and over because they did not record the solutions the first time. It is not acceptable to not know if their plan is correct or if it is working at all. It is not acceptable to lose in a final to someone keeping a Performance Journal. It is not acceptable to lose because they're just too lazy to do what is needed to win.

For many years I fought the concept of keeping a Performance Journal. I worked hard in training, and I wanted to eliminate any unnecessary work. Still, it was not until I discovered a productive journal-keeping system that my training and match scores improved and were much more consistent. With a journal, I was able to review my progress and better evaluate my efforts using a systematic approach to record keeping. The system I created is called "Performance Analysis".

Performance Analysis is the process of recording in your Performance Journal essential information that tracks your progress. It is a complete system, taking only a few minutes a day, which utilizes positive reinforcement to build Self-Image and speed the writer toward their goal. You should use a page or two for each day, with sufficient space to enter the needed data. The purpose of the journal is to add organization to a training program, not burden your child with unnecessary work.

Performance Analysis, the journal we recommend and sell, is designed to do all of these things, and to grow the Self-Image circle at the same time. Our journal is in a durable book format that is easy to use and inexpensive to purchase. It is available on our website at www.mentalmanagementstore.com or by calling our offices at 972-899-9640.

The Elements of a Performance Journal

Our Performance Analysis Journal contains a written record of six key planning areas:

Competition Log

Equipment Log

General Data Section

Solution Analysis

Success Analysis

Daily Goal Statement

Competition and Equipment Log

The Competition Log records the game dates, results, and page numbers for the journal entries of games. The Equipment Log records all the equipment being used. You only make entries in this log when changing, adding, or repairing equipment.

General Data Section

The General Data Section records what you did. Fill in the date, location, event (training or competition), weather, and the time of day and duration of the activity. Next, write down exactly what you learned and what you accomplished during this period. How many attempts did you make? How many hours did you train? How did you spend the time? What was the result or score? If you do not train or compete on a day or do anything that affects your sport or activity, do not fill out a journal page.

> Three swimmers meet at a swimming pool. One sits in the sun, never entering the water. The second puts her feet in the water but does not leave the poolside. The third swims twenty laps in the pool. Later, all three will say they were swimming that day.

It is easy for us to say we are training when in fact we are spending most of our time visiting with other competitors, setting up equipment, or wasting time. A good journal entry eliminates rationalizations and just records the facts.

Solution Analysis

The Solution Analysis section records what was learned. The writer documents any solutions to challenges they have discovered during a training day. If a problem occurs and the player does not know the proper solution, simply state, "I'm looking for a solution to....," and then describe the problem. This section aids your kids in focusing on solutions instead of problems. Writing down the solution to issues will reduce the chance that they will repeat in the future.

Success Analysis

In the Success Analysis section, they should write down anything they did well during a day of training, thereby improving the probability they will repeat the success. If they set a personal record, this section should be lengthy and descriptive. The journal forces the user to learn from mistakes and reinforce successful efforts. We are not accustomed to bragging about ourselves, but that is precisly what your kids should do in this section. Be honest, but go out of the way to reinforce in writing every good performance. That's what the Top 5% do.

Goal Statement

The goal statement is the best way to close the journal page. They should state a goal they intend to reach. Write it in the first person present tense, as if they have already achieved it. Some examples of goals statements are:

I often shoot above 390/400.

I am on the United States Olympic team.

I often shoot below par.

I am the most consistent player on our team.

Goal statements should be achievements that are currently out of reach, but not out of sight. Every time they write down a goal, they are that much closer to its attainment. Only two things are possible. The goal is reached, or you will stop writing it down. As long as they continue to write down goal statements, they are moving toward their attainment.

Performance Analysis is one of the most useful coaching tools. You can learn much from reviewing your child's journal. A correctly written Performance Journal provides the athlete, the coach, and the parent with a valuable resource for improvement, without burdening, unnecessary paperwork.

Chapter 10

Dealing With Pressure

"How can I avoid the pressure I feel when competing?" This question, or something like it, is likely to be asked of you by your child at some point. In fact, I might have asked that same question early in my career to my dad. All kids are conditioned to the commonly held idea that pressure is a bad thing. If it's bad, then we need to avoid it.

That idea presented a problem for me because every time I competed in a big competition, I felt pressure. I didn't feel it in training very often. Interestingly enough, it did not seem to cause my scores to go down, but it presented me with concern and caused increased anxiety when it occurred. In my more than 50 years as both a competitor and a coach, I have known only a few athletes declaring they do not feel competitive stress. For many, the effects of pressure are destructive causing loss of points at critical times. A few credited pressure with the premature termination of their career. A surprising number of elite performers find that the pressure of competition is useful, even essential, to the attainment of their best performances.

Pressure is a state of mental or emotional strain or tension resulting from adverse or very demanding circumstances and is a regular part of life. Your kids experience it often. Remember how you felt when the teacher called on you in class? Did you stress out over an exam or a presentation before the class? I did. Competition pressure is the same song, different verse.

Here is the best answer I can offer you as a parent to the question of avoiding pressure.

"Pressure is not something you need to avoid. It is something you need to control."

To control something, we must first understand it. You can hear kids complaining about butterflies, being uncomfortable, fearful, or the infamous choke. We hear people talking about pressuring out in a stressful situation but never pressuring in. We seem to have a great vocabulary for the harmful effects of pressure and few words for the helpful ones. Pressure, simply put, is neither positive nor negative. Pressure is like air. Too much and you have a hurricane. Too little and you suffocate. But in the correct amount, it is the breath of life.

There is a great example, and maybe you've

heard of it. Let's imagine there is an I-beam on the floor, the kind they use for construction. It looks kind of like an H made out of metal they use to give some strength to buildings. Let's say it is about 20' long and 5 inches wide and it's laying the ground. So, it kind of looks like a railroad rail. You're not going to have any problem standing on this or walking on it. Somebody says, "Hey, I'll pay you $100 if you walk from one end to the other, turn around and walk back without falling off." You'll probably have no problem doing that. Your Self-Image will probably say, "Yeah, it's like me to do this. I can easily do this." So you walk down and back with no problem at all and get your $100.

If somebody were to ask, "What you were picturing when you walked that beam." You were probably thinking about the $100 – it's no big deal, it's easy enough for you to transverse this and it is the easiest $100 you have ever made.

But let's take that same I-beam and let's put it 150 feet up off the ground and see if you want to walk it now for $100. I would venture to say that unless you're a high-wire walker or somebody who has done high steel work, you're probably going to decline. Now, if you had to walk it, would you be thinking about the $100? I doubt it; you'd probably be thinking about what happens if I fall. Now you have something to lose, and the pressure goes way up. Let's look at how your three mental processes handle this situation. On the ground, the Conscious mind was thinking about the $100 gained. Up in the air, it is thinking about falling. Change what you picture, and you feel something different inside. You tighten up. Pressure takes its toll. Your Subconscious skill did not change. You have the ability to walk a 5" wide 20' long beam whether it is on the ground or in the air. But look what happens to your Self-Image? Is it like you to risk your life for a $100? No way!

We Need Pressure

The fact is we need pressure. We just need it in the right amount. I've spent 40 years trying to understand it so I can use it to an advantage. Here's what I've come up with; pressure is two things at the same time, Anxiety and Tension.

Anxiety

Anxiety is fear. It is almost always viewed as a negative. But, think about it. Fear keeps me from driving too fast, following too close to the car in front of me, and causes me to look both ways at an intersection. Fear in a competition can be paralyzing to the uninformed, and that is unfortunate. Here is the good news, fear dissipates with experience. I've got to admit I was scared in my first nationals as a junior. But, the second one was easier.

Someone once said the final in the Olympics is the greatest pressure situation a person can face short of a loss of life encounter. I might add that pressure also increases in direct proportion to your chances of winning. I've been there, and I agree. I was favored to win the gold in Montreal in 1976, but I did not feel fear. I did feel tension.

Tension

That is the other side of pressure. Tension is your kid's level of excitement. Everything they do well has a corresponding amount of anticipation. If they are too relaxed, they become careless. If they are too nervous, they hesitate. People have a natural Tension State. Some are calm by nature while others are bouncing off of the walls most of the time. Sports also have different optimal Tension States. Sports like fencing and downhill skiing are high excitement activities. These athletes are excited and full of adrenaline from the start. Archery and golf are low tension sports. International Rifle is just above coma. Adrenaline, a hormone secreted by the adrenal glands, especially in conditions of stress, increasing rates of blood circulation, breathing, and carbohydrate metabolism preparing muscles for exertion. It increases the pulse rate and moves the excitement level up. Way up! However, again this is not all bad. An adrenaline push can cause increased endurance, added strength, and greater awareness of the senses.

So, if your child is a naturally high excitement person in a low tension sport, they may have more trouble with stress control than someone more naturally balanced to their sport. If that is the case, some proven techniques must be learned, practiced and mastered to help control the unwanted excitement.

If your child is too nervous in a competition, I have some suggestions that can help to match their excitement level to their activity.

Recognize that pressure is positive and something that they can control.

1. Pressure is not imagined. Your young performer must learn to accept it is okay to feel something different in a pressure situation. Their body is saying, "This is important. Pay attention!" It is important to accept the advantages of stress and expect their scores will be better for having felt pressure. Also, do not be surprised if they occasionally do not notice pressure's effects even in a big competition. Pressure does not always make itself known to the Conscious Mind.

Focus on what you want to see happen not on what is stressing you.

2. Most of the time when performers experience point-reducing pressure it's because they are thinking about something that causes the level to rise. "Boy, I really need this one!" "What am I doing wrong?" "If I finish this series well I win the match" These thoughts are on outcomes, not on the process of performing. Thinking about what they are doing wrong or counting their score just increases the adverse effects of tension. Tell them to keep their mind on the process of executing well, and the outcome will take care of itself.

Use a practiced recovery strategy.

3. Sometimes the pressure seems to increase just after an unfortunate series, and they might need a way to recover. One useful technique is to have a planned and trained recovery strategy. All recovery strategies have two important things in common. First, they must get their mind off of the things increasing the pressure. Secondly, they must do something that they can control. Here is an example. They've had a bad series of shots, and begin to think about the score, and they need to recover. First, concentrate on breathing. Breathe in a practiced pattern for say three breaths. Then relax a particular muscle group such as their neck and shoulders. Finally, visualize being in complete control of performing well. They can only think of one thing at a time so while thinking helpful thoughts they cannot be still thinking negatively. Also, a person can 100% control their method of breathing, the relaxation of their muscles, and the visualization, so the second step is accomplished as well. Now, when they refocus on their next series, they should be recovered and perform well.

Learn to fake a yawn.

4. A final recommendation might seem strange, but this works. If your young performers find themselves becoming a bit too nervous and need a quick tool to get calmed down, suggest they try yawning. That's right. Do a FAKE YAWN. The same chemicals that cause the muscles to relax when we yawn naturally, also seem to work just the same when fak-

ing one. Next time you watch the Olympics on TV watch for this technique. You will see someone in a pressure situation yawning. Everyone else will think he is really in control. You will know the truth. He might be using the fake yawn to control unwanted pressure.

OK, so what is the bottom line on Pressure? First of all, let your kids know it is OK to feel it. When I was first competing, I had the idea that every time I felt a little something in my stomach, and my hands got sweaty, my score was always going to go down. I believed experiencing the external effects of pressure was a sign of weakness and a result of not having trained properly. World and Olympic Champions do not feel pressure. Right?

All of those ideas were wrong. When I interviewed Olympic gold medalists for two years right after the 1972 Olympics, I found out they all felt nervous at the Olympics. No one ever got to the point that training and experience totally eliminated feeling nervous, but their attitude about pressure was different than mine in my first Olympiad. Their attitude was, "Oh yeah, I feel my stomach turn over, and my hands get sweaty. Isn't that great? It just makes winning more fun." When you overcome the feeling of pressure, when you perform well under pressure, there's no better feeling than that. I realized I did not want to eliminate the very thing that could enhance the joy of winning, I needed to embrace it.

"Remember, coal under pressure produces a diamond. Performers in control under pressure produce winning scores."-Henry Kissinger

Chapter 11

Rehearsal, The Most Versatile Mental Tool

Imagery, visualization, and mental rehearsal are common ways to refer to the process of thinking about an action without physically doing it. In this chapter, we will look at this method, why it works and why it is the most versatile and often used mental tool.

I like the term rehearsal over visualization or imagery just because it is a simple name. Many good things would lose their meaning if the terms used to describe them seem complicated. Rehearsal is not complex in the way I am using it. All of us have used Rehearsal. Remember rehearsing your lines in the school play, that Bible verse you had to memorize, or the first lines of a speech you had to make in school. Your children are experts at rehearsal, and without ever being taught they can visualize winning races, slaying dragons and becoming champions.

Thinking about doing a task is much easier to

do than actually doing it. I won the Olympics thousands of times in my mind before entering the competition in Montreal in 1976. I believe this rehearsal imprinted my Self-Image to accept that the challenge of winning was like me to do.

There is no perfect way to do it. Some clients tell me they see vivid colors and hear sounds, the world slows down and becomes clearer. Well, I cannot relate to that. My rehearsal is a little blurry, and I do not hear sounds at all, but it took me to the Olympic Gold anyway. I am open to the idea that the more vivid your rehearsal, the greater the effect. I also believe the more often you rehearse the more useful it becomes, but I do not think you have to see colors or sounds to be able to have effective rehearsal. It can be done in a few seconds, or take minutes or even hours to complete. You can do it on or off of the field, while you are exercising, sitting up or lying down, while you are waiting for someone or for something to occur. It is not only easy to do, but it is FREE.

How Rehearsal Works

Rehearsal aids your young performer in executing the desired action or move with precision. I was interested in knowing why this works, and after a bit of research, I discovered when you vividly rehearse a task, you create neural pathways in the brain. Small tracks engraved in the brain cells ultimately enable an athlete to perform the action subconsciously. Therefore, one of the benefits of rehearsal is it paves the roadways that we must travel to perform the desired task. (Porter, K., Foster, J. Visual Athletics. Dubuque, Iowa: Wm. C. Publishers, 1990)

Shane Murphy, one of the sports psychologists at the Olympic Training Center while I lived in Colorado Springs along with Robert L. Woolfolk and Mark W. Parrish conducted an interesting study related to performance and rehearsal. Here is the essense of the study.

An investigation was carried out to evaluate the effect of imagery instructions on a simple motor skill accuracy task (putting a golf ball). Thirty college students were blocked on their putting ability and randomly assigned within blocks to one of three experimental conditions: (a) positive imagery, (b) negative imagery, and (c) control.

Subjects in the two imagery conditions were given the same instructions for imagining the backswing and putting stroke. In the positive imagery group, subjects imagined the ball going into the cup, while subjects using negative imagery visualized the ball narrowly missing the hole. Subjects in the control group putted without instructions. On each of six consecutive days, a 10-putt trial was conducted for each subject.

There was a significant effect on performance improvement. Analyses showed significant differences among all groups, with positive imagery producing the most improvement, the control condition producing less, and negative imagery resulting in performance deterioration.

Is this proof that rehearsal works? It sure looks like it. I think it is interesting that the negative imagery group's performance went down over the test period while the positive rehearsal group's performance increased. I have observed this occurring repeatedly with my clients over my 40 years as a performance coach. Not only does positive imagery increase performance, but when your kids think about creating error they improve the chance of the error occurring as well. When they worry that bad things might happen to them, they are rehearsing them. They are building new neural pathways toward failure.

Rehearsal as Mental Practice

Rehearsal is mental practice, and it has many advantages for your young performer. First, they are mentally duplicating everything they do when they perform without having to exert physical effort, expending resources, or needing anyone's assistance. The golfer, as an example, does not need to go anywhere, purchase range or course fees, and never has to look for a lost ball. It's cheap. It costs absolutely nothing, and you can do it anytime. Also, by rehearsing only good performances, there is no negative reinforcement. Mental practice is a bargain and done correctly is powerfully effective.

You can imagine far more than you currently can achieve. If you consistently rehearse what you want to attain, what you imagine can become a reality.

Let me give you an example from my book *With Winning in Mind.* Back in the 1970s, I was shooting well in the kneeling stage of the competition and began approaching the national record of 396/400. I wanted to set the record at 400, a perfect score. But I had never actually fired a 400, even in training. Nonetheless, an hour a day for two weeks, I vividly rehearsed shooting the first 100, then another and another. I visualized each of the last ten shots building toward the record. I rehearsed what I knew would happen at that point: I would realize that I was above the record. Next, I rehearsed hearing a voice say, "That's OK, I do this all the time," Then I imagined shooting the final ten easily and saying to myself, "Another 400, that's like me."

In my first competition since beginning the rehearsal, I started with a 100 kneeling. My next two targets were also 100s. I started my last series with ten, ten, ten, ten, ten. Only five more to go. I shot three more tens then the environment began to talk to me.. I was above the record. I heard an internal voice say, "That's OK, I do this all the time." I shot two additional tens, setting the national record at a perfect 400.

In our next chapter, I will show you how rehearsal plays a part in the Mental Process we teach our clients at Mental Management Systems.

Chapter 12

What To Do When Things Go Wrong

Perhaps no time is more important for you to know what to say to your children than when they come home after a disappointing performance.

I'll do my best to tell you what to do and more importantly what not to do, but I wish I could say I was good at this while my kids were young. My wife Helen was the parenting expert. I'm confident I violated every rule in this book, but maybe I can save you from repeating my mistakes.

> *"Most of the things that happen to your kids that they view as a negative are both necessary and desirable."*

It is your job to show them this is true. I warn you; children resist this procedure.

The Three Magic Questions

Building Self-Image in your kids should be a primary goal for every parent, but most do not know where to start. It begins in the Reinforcement Phase of the task. Remember, the Anticipation Phase of a task is a Conscious issue, the Action Phase relates to the Subconscious, and the Reinforcement Phase either builds or tears down the Self-Image.

The first conversation a performer has after a task is a special one. The Self-Image imprints best just after the completion of a task. One of the worst things a parent can ask their young performer after a game or event is "How did you do?" This question seems harmless until you look at it in the context of what it is doing to the Self-Image. "How did you do?" is an open-ended question. We live in a negatively charged world; chances are your child will talk about what they did wrong before they get to what they did right. A negative response is the common one. Asking the question this way opens the door for a negative Imprint. You did not mean to, but you have possibly created a harmful Imprint in their Self-Image, and at the most damaging time.

Using what I call the Magic Three Questions will prevent the chance for a negative Imprint and guarantees a positive one. I am a performance coach, and we train elite coaches, managers, and teachers here at Mental Management Systems, who are often the first person their performer talks to after an event. We teach them to ask the following three questions.

"What did you do well?"

"What did you learn?"

"What are you going to do about it?"

I want my athletes to imprint their successful efforts immediately after they finish, improving the chance of becoming "like them" to repeat them in the future. Do you pick up your child after their performances? You are the most important performance coach in your child's life, and you want them to talk first about what they did well. There are many ways to ask this question.

"What did you enjoy?"

"Tell me about the best part of that game?"

"What was fun today?"

Let's look at the second question. Only two things should happen when competing: you win, or you learn. There is no winning and losing. When any part of an attempt goes well, that's a win. The place on the leaderboard or the final score on the scoreboard matters not. It is a win! But, when something goes wrong, they will want to tell you about it. Every time you talk about an error you improve the chance of making it in the future. A better approach would be to discuss the solution to the mistake and not the error itself. I recognize it is often necessary to address the problem to get to the solution, but please try to get there as soon as possible. One way to guide the conversation is to ask them, "What did you learn?" or "What do you think this is teaching you?" Making mistakes is one of the best ways to learn and in some cases, it is the only way. It is not a mental error to make a mistake if you learn from it.

Finally, you want your performers to tell you what they are going to do about what just happened. Hopefully, they will seek the solution to concerns and work diligently to correct them.

Respond, Not React

You should not expect your children to be happy after a poor performance. Your goal should be to help them respond to mistakes instead of reacting to them. The key is to help them control the Imprinting and protect the Self-Image at this most vulnerable time.

You begin by giving them something to think about that builds Self-Image to replace thinking about what they did wrong which harms their Self-Image. Remember, picturing the solution causes the Self-Image to grow; imagining the problem causes it to shrink.

I am not saying we should never think about the problem. But, it is vital to isolate the area that needs improvement. Many young performers tend to see themselves as total failures after making a mistake in only one area of their performance. The key for Mom and Dad is to help their young performer see the error for what it is and not beat themselves up. Most mistakes in a competition fall into four areas. Strategical, Technical, Environmental, and Mental. One successful strategy is to ask the question, "Do you think you can narrow your performance down by evaluating how you did in the following categories?"Let's look at examples of each one.

Fixing Strategical Errors

Strategical Errors are Anticipation Phase and Action Phase issues, happening before and during the action. They include preparing appropriately for the task and making the best choices during the game. Sometimes Strategical Errors are unavoidable. Here are some examples. A running back chooses the wrong path on a run, and is stopped for a loss. The execution failed because of a poor choice, but if he chose what he thought was the best option available to him, should he count this as an error? A baseball player while on first base decides to steal second base and fails. You do not know if a decision like this one will work until you try it. A golfer misreads a putt. Determining the best line is not an exact science even for the pros. The suggestion a parent should make to reducing Strategical Errors is to ask your child, "If you could do this play over, how would you want it to go? What would you do differently?" Get them talking about the solution, not the problem.

Fixing Technical Errors

Technical Errors relate to the Action Phase of a Task, occurring during the action. A quarterback overthrows a receiver. An infielder misses the tag on a runner in baseball. A golfer hits a shot out of bounds. A soccer player kicks the ball wide of the goal. A tennis player hits a shot in the net. Technical Errors are the easiest to see but are often caused by Mental, Strategical or Environmental Error. When your child is concerned about a Technical Error, ask "What do you do when you execute this action well?" Get them talking about the solution, not the problem.

Fixing Environmental Errors

Environmental Errors can be Action Phase or Reinforcement Phase issues. Reacting inappropriately to the actions of others, making an error because of the actions of others, or making an error because of the environment itself. A kicker in a football game misses a field goal because of his holder's mistake. A first baseman misses a catch from the shortstop because of a poor throw. A soccer player loses her footing and falls on a slippery field. Someone calls your child a name or offends them in some way. When your child is concerned about an Environmental Error, ask "Is there anything you could have done to make this situation better? If not, the best thing is to dismiss it. Just let it go." Get them to recognize when they are not the problem; they are not to worry.

Fixing Mental Errors

Empowering you to help your kids seek solutions to common Mental Error issues is the major focus of this book. Mental Errors can happen at any time and are often the cause of other types of errors. They include thinking harmful instead of helpful thoughts, failing to learn when making mistakes, over-trying, over-thinking, worrying about what other people think, self-centeredness, losing focus, beating yourself up, disrespecting rules and those in authority, lack of work ethic, getting angry over a bad result, having doubt or lack of belief in one's ability or choices.

I find in working with my students, Environmental, Technical, and Strategical errors are often the result of a Mental error. Thinking a distracting thought immediately before a critical action could cause a loss of focus, leading to a reduced Technical performance. Beating yourself up over one poor attempt could cause the next one to repeat the error. If you surround yourself with negative people, soon you will become just like them. Worrying about making mistakes improves the probability of making them.

Parents become aware of mental errors when problems surface. Perhaps they observe a problem, or the young performer informs them of a mistake they committed. When your children begin to tell you about problems they are having you become their mental coach. How effectively your kids deal with mental error is directly influenced by your attitude about problems.

Are Problems a Problem?

I think most kids view negative outcomes the way I did as a young competitor. Life would be better if I did not have any. Now, with the benefit of years of experience, I've come to a different opinion.

Almost every valuable thing I've learned in my life has come from learning from mistakes.

"Making mistakes is inevitable, learning from them is a choice."

In this section, I hope to make the case that adverse outcomes are an essential part of success in competition. In fact, if you can impart this truth to your kids, much of life's frustration will pass them by.

Problems Identify Areas for Growth

In my first year on my university shooting team, I set a goal to become First-Team All-American in the Three-Position Smallbore Rifle event. The top ten collegiate shooters in America receive this award. When hearing the news, I received Second-Team status; I was disappointed. After careful evaluation of the possible reasons I made Second-Team, I determined my kneeling scores were a bit lower than the top shooters. I talked to my father, still my coach at that time, about a possible solution.

"To find an effective solution you need to understand the cause of the problem," he said. I thought I knew what the problem was; I was not shooting kneeling as well as my standing and prone positions.

"I know the cause," I said. "I'm not a great kneeling shooter. I don't like kneeling. It is uncomfortable to shoot.

" If you continue with that attitude where will it take you?"

After a long pause, I said, "Nowhere." I did not realize the cause of my problem was more of my attitude about kneeling than my ability to shoot well in the position. Attitude is a Self-Image issue.

"I can fix your kneeling, but you won't do it," he said.

My father knew me well enough to know this was a challenge I would be unable to turn down.

"I'll do it, if it will get me First-Team next year," I replied.

Dad challenged me to dry-fire kneeling one hour every day for the three months between semesters. I did not want to do it, but I was determined to show him I was up to his challenge. So, each evening before I went to bed I donned my shooting clothes, assumed the kneeling position with my rifle and simulated shooting for an hour. I never missed a night. By the start of the next semester, my kneeling scores were among the best in the country. Kneeling became my favorite stage of competition throughout my career. I made First-Team All-American the remaining three years.

Having a Self-Image of "I do not like kneeling" hindered my acquiring the needed Subconscious skills necessary to reach my goal. The Self-Image of "It is like me to show my dad I can do the task of dry firing" meant more to me than not liking kneeling. The result was an essential change in behavior. I did not understand, at the young age of 19, overcoming obstacles is how we grow, but my father did.

Problems Determine the Price

"People Appreciate Things in Direct Proportion to the Price They Pay for Them."-Vince Lombardi

One of the reasons winning is so sweet is because it is so hard to do. We tend to value things in direct proportion to the price we pay for them. This principle is valid for your kids as well. What if winning was easy for them. What if there were no exams, and everyone got an A. What if there were no grades, no prizes, no victors, no medalists, no champions. When you eliminate the need to reward excellence, I think there might be less reason to get better, little need to overcome obstacles or seek solutions to problems.

Anything your kids work for, they will value, Look for ways to allow them to have an investment in the task. When they earn their way, pride is enhanced. When too many things are given to them, they tend to become entitled.

Also, a child's Self-Image may increase when they choose to do things with no thought of reward or recognition. When they go out of their way to help someone unnoticed, the reward is internal. Perhaps, this is the greatest value you can place on a task; to do something well because that is who you are, not because you are being paid or recognized for it.

I have often heard our American society may be creating an entitlement culture. I fear because our ancestors suffered in the building this great country, desiring to make life better and easier for their children, every generation has had fewer problems to overcome, and has lost some of the appreciation for paying the price. We may have created the idea in some that hard work, excellence, and earning your way is being replaced by half-way effort, let's lower the standards, and a someone should give it to me attitude.

We live in different times when in a certain Texas high school, students who earned the right to wear National Honor Society stoles at graduation, were informed by the school they would not be allowed to wear them because it is not inclusive of all students. - June 1, 2016, Fox News

I hope you can motivate your children to become excellent. Do they want the doctor who operates on them in the future to have attended an easy medical school? Do they want the soldier defending their country or the policeman answering the call to have low standards in their training? If they become a business owner, do they want the workers they hire to expect a high wage without providing skilled service? Do they really want the tasks required by the sports they compete in and the classes in school to be easy ones?

Problems create obstacles in the way of your child's success. Problems force them to make a choice: ignore the problem, be defeated by it, or overcome it. Their self-worth is at stake. Every time they solve a problem or overcome an obstacle their Self-Image grows. Making it easy today always makes it harder tomorrow.

Problems and Fearlessness

Being fearful they will not do well in the competition, that they will be disappointed, or miss out on the joy of winning is widespread among competitors, young and old. No one wants to lose a game, let down their team, or be the one last to cross the finish line. This fear can be a motivator to work more diligently in preparation for the event. That's a good thing. But this form of anxiety can also be destructive if we are fearful in the competition. To imagine we are going to perform poorly creates an imprint in our Self-Image that it is "like us" to fail. We tend to become what we imprint. That is a bad thing!

So what are we to do about this potentially destructive form of motivation? I offer this suggestion. Tell your kids to go into competition with the attitude that everything that happens in the event is for their benefit. Tell them: "Only two things can happen to you; you win, or you learn. There is no lose." We tend to learn more when we struggle and make mistakes than when everything goes well. I am not against having a flawless performance, but

I am suggesting we learn more from our errors and poor performances than we do from our good ones. There is great value in learning from error. I have never met a winner that has not failed many times and learned from the failures. The key is to learn, not to fear. Their future will be full of fearful times. Turn problems into opportunities to grow. Competition is practice for the game of life. Tell your kids the most important things about competing are to learn more about themselves, how the respond to pressure, and get better today than yesterday.

It is possible to be fearless in any event if you teach your children to accept these three principles.

1. Everything that happens to you in a competition needs to happen.

2. Only two things can happen to you; you win, or you learn.

3. If there is no possible adverse outcome, there is no reason to be fearful.

Problems and Other People

Comparing to Others

Thoughts about other competitors are one of the leading causes of damage to the Self-Image of performers. The minute your kids think about another player, the possibility of a comparison to themselves starts. Several imprints are possible at this point. "He is better than me. I am better than him. We are about equal to each other." If your child suspects she is a better player than the majority of her competition, her Self-Image will likely grow because of the comparison. But, the opposite is also true. Being in a group of superiors tends to remind a person they are not as good as the others. This situation might cause a drop in Self-Image.

I've also observed you tend to become like the people around you. If you play with more accomplished athletes, you tend to improve. Why are both of these observations true? The key is in the Imprinting.

If your child, when they are around superiors, think about what they do not have, their Self-Image shrinks. If, however, they choose to picture what they could become the Self-Image grows. It is a choice.

As a young baseball player, I thought about all of the things wrong with me. I was slow, short, and a bit lacking in the hand-to-eye skills. Consequently, my Self-Image got smaller every time I thought about the other players. I thought only about what I lacked. By the time I arrived at the US Army Marksmanship Unit, with a history of seeing myself at the top of the leader board in college, I was motivated by those better than me. I began to think only about what I could become. Helping your kids make the right choice in this situation is critical to their success in life.

Worrying About What Other People Say

This issue has increased exponentially with the growth of the Internet, cell phones, forums, Twitter, and Facebook. In my teenage days, we had one phone in the house and wrote letters that took days to get there. If someone said something bad about me on Friday, I did not find out about it until school on Monday. By that time, most issues had resolved themselves. Today, everything is recordable, videoable, textable, and instantly deliverable. Both the frequency and intensity of comments increase with the availability of technology. The chances your kids will be offended by someone or something is unavoidable. As a parent, it is common to see your athletes performance negatively affected by the comments of the people they are around. When your kids come to you with this issue, you can bet it has risen to a high level of concern for them. Small offenses go away by themselves. So, what are you to do?

I'd like to offer a few suggestions for your consideration. First, hear them out. The fact your kids are coming to you when they are hurting is huge. Not all parents have their children confiding in them. Although talking about their problems is a negative Imprint on their Self-Image, this is one time when it may be advisable to allow it. There is a big difference between beating themselves up after a bad performance and feeling offended by another person, especially if the one doing the offending is someone important in their eyes. The first issue is a mental error that is self-generated, correctable by choosing to think about the solution to the poor performance. The second is much more complicated. I suggest asking your young performer several questions at this point. First, "Has this happened before?" If this is a single incidence, there is a good chance it is a misunderstanding. Next, "How does it make you feel?" Once the feelings are out in the open, it is often possible to suggest the following.

Tell them to go to the person that offended them and say.

"Here is what I heard you say."

"This is how it made me feel."

"Is that what you intended?"

I have used this approach many times with my athletes with success. Most of the time it solves the problem between teammates, siblings, and competitors.

Dealing with Negative People

Wouldn't it be great if everyone you came in contact with were positive and encouraging? Not happening you say? Chances are excellent it is the same with your children as well. Some people are complainers, finding fault with everything. When your son or daughter hears another person complain, the Self-Images of both people are negatively Imprinted. If they stay around people complaining about a topic long enough, your children will become complainers.

Athletes at the top of their game tend to shut out the damaging effects of negative talk. Here is an example.

Your son is on the school golf team, playing in a tournament. A member of his foursome is disturbed about hitting his ball in the trap and says, "That hurts! I hate it when I have to play a bunker shot." I'm suggesting you tell your son to handle this situation the way the pros do; after you hear a person whine about a shot, imprint the positive result in your mind. Hear yourself say, "I'm great bunker player!" Answer a negative Imprint with a positive one.

This technique works for any negative thought. Answer it with the opposite one.

How to Beat Worry

Instead of picturing what might go wrong, think about what you want to happen. Here are some more examples.

" I am worried I might do poorly on the upcoming exam."

Change it to "I'm going to do great on that test."

"If I do not play well my team might lose the game."

"We are going to win because I will play well."

Dealing with Disappointing You

One of the primary fears in your children, as they compete, is the fear of disappointing you. Your kids fear they will not do well in a competition, and you will be displeased with them. No one wants to lose a game or be the one last to cross the finish line, but they must not see the disappointment in your eyes.

So what are we to do about this situation? I offer this suggestion. Teach them to go into competition with the attitude that everything that happens in the event is OK with you. Only two things can happen to them; they win, or they learn, **but you always have their back.** There is no disappointed Mom or Dad. We tend to bond more with our children when they struggle and make mistakes than when everything goes well. Knowing what to do when things go great is easy. Everyone is happy. But, there is great value in learning from error together. I have never met a winner that has not failed many times and learned from the failures, often together with Mom and Dad. The key is to learn not to fear. Life is full of fearful times, turn these into opportunities to grow. The most important thing about competing is who you become, not where you finish. Teach them not to let fear become an obstacle to the opportunity they have to learn something valuable about themselves. Take advantage of the times when your kids fail; see it as a chance for you to be there with them to discover a way to succeed.

Over-Trying

Jane is a good tennis player. Her skills are solid enough to beat her competition. Her equipment is the finest money can buy, and no one works harder in training. She should win, but she doesn't. John plays well in smaller competitions but when he gets to ones that are important to him he has trouble performing well. He should win, but he doesn't.

So what is the reason? In my more than 40 years of competing and coaching there is one factor that is most often the culprit. It takes more points from those that are skilled and have trained diligently than any other. The villain is the amount of mental effort the player uses in the tournament.

"Giving all you've got, giving 110%, and trying as hard as you can, is almost guaranteed to keep you from winning."

When your kids give it their all, they may be trying too hard. If their level of mental effort exceeds the optimum, they lose points. Let's look at why this happens and what you can do to help them.

When we begin any form of skill acquisition, we are forced to do things consciously. An example would be looking at the keys when starting to learn to type. I have to admit that I still have to look at the numbers when typing, but the keys are touched automatically now that I've been at it for a good while. As my Conscious mind can only think about one thing at a time, I was slow as Christmas at typing in the beginning. As I began to practice, interesting things happened. Soon I found I didn't have to think about the keys. They seem to type without conscious effort. When this happens, we are typing with our Subconscious mind. What a difference! Our speed increases and so does our enjoyment of the skill of typing.

Skill acquisition in performance occurs the same way. At first, we have to think about the elements of our form. Through training, we begin to do them automatically or Subconsciously. There is a huge advantage when the Subconscious controls the action. The Conscious mind can only think of one thing a time while the Subconscious can handle many activities simultaneously. We perform best when the Conscious mind is quiet, and the Subconscious is in control.

So if this is true, why would we ever want to play Consciously? We shouldn't. But, we do this every time we try too hard in competition. It has been my observation that close to 90% of all athletes are trying too hard in their matches. Amazing isn't it? Here's why. When we get to a significant competition, we naturally want to perform well. The Conscious mind can override the Subconscious at will. So, the Conscious mind, to insure a successful outcome, overrides the Subconscious. The result is a drop in scores and an unhappy player.

Over-trying doesn't happen in practice or unimportant competitions because the Conscious mind is happy to let the Subconscious take over in lesser situations. You see, the ego resides in the Conscious mind. It seems to resent not being in charge when the critical events in life occur. Also, it appears that the Subconscious is quite willing to allow the Conscious mind to take over its job any time it desires. The Subconscious is the team we want on the field. We need for the Conscious to stay on the bench but if it takes the field, we will have a difficult time winning the game.

So, if this happens to your kids, what are they to do? We need for the Conscious to do just enough and no more. Everything in life requires a certain amount of effort to perform well. Give it one percent less mental attention than is necessary and performance drops. That's being CARELESS. Give it one percent MORE mental effort, and again performance drops. That's being CAREFUL.

How can you tell if the effort your kids are using is too much? If a thought crosses their mind of desperately needing a particular outcome, or score begins to dominate their thinking, they may be over-trying. Giving it all you've got in a competition is over-trying. Over-trying is so prevalent I believe most athletes are doing it in every competition, and do not know what it feels like to give the activity the correct amount of effort. If they were to try just hard enough, their performance would not suffer from this error. But, because they want to do well, they Over-try.

When a performer is doing well in training, but cannot duplicate the performance in a competition, the most likely cause is over-trying. It has cost many a good athlete a higher place on the leader board and has even terminated careers prematurely. Ironically, those who seem most susceptible to this error are the most conscientious and hard working among us.

What is the right amount of mental effort? I asked this question to hundreds of elite performers, and this is the best answer I've received.

"The optimum level of mental effort and let's just have fun today are close together."

That's right! There is a time to try hard, but it is not in the competition. The time to TRY is in preparation, not in execution. We must TRUST in execution. That's correct. TRUST! Trust your training. If you are not training effectively, you will have a difficult time in having anything to trust in a competition.

Unfortunately, most players TRY in execution, and that is the problem. You might try the following statements when your child over-tries.

"How hard would you have to try if you knew you would do well? Think about it. You could enjoy the experience if there were no fear of an adverse outcome."

*"That is exactly the feeling you should have
when competing. Relax and let it happen, don't try to make it happen. Making
it happen is putting the Conscious mind on
the field and over-trying results. Just let it
happen. Trust your Subconscious. Let it do
its job."*

Quieting the Conscious mind while in the act of
performing is not an easy task. Most athletes find
if they do not give the Conscious mind something
helpful to think about, it will find harmful things on
its own. It has been my experience if the Conscious
mind is not occupied or quiet, it almost always over-
powers the Subconscious, and trying too hard is the
result.

So, what should your kids think about in a competition? I teach my students to think about execution, not outcome or score. Ask them, when they
are performing well what are they picturing? If this
thought pattern can be defined, it can be duplicated in
competition instead of allowing a potentially harmful series of thoughts to damage their chance of doing well. It is possible to define a series of thoughts
that work; we call this running a Mental Program.

Running a Mental Program is such an individual
thing that I hesitate to recommend what you should
think about in a book. However, I can suggest that
their Mental Program should occupy the Conscious
mind, trigger the Subconscious to perform the action well and be duplicable. If they run their Mental
Program and have the attitude that they are going to

enjoy the process of playing, it will go a long way to avoid over-trying in big competitions.

Overcoming

"Where you finish does not always measure how far you've come."

Olympic history abounds with tales of athletes who overcame crippling adversity to win gold medals. Karoly Takacs of Hungary is one of those. Takacs, a right-handed shooter was part of Hungary's world champion pistol shooting team in 1938. As a soldier in the Hungarian army, Takacs suffered a tragic blow when a grenade exploded taking his right hand off at the wrist. Takacs had a goal set to win the Olympics and would not be derailed. He learned to load and shoot with his left hand. Ten years later in 1948, Karoly won his first gold medal in rapid-fire pistol shooting with his left hand. In 1952, he would repeat as Olympic Champion.

Canadian Silken Laumann was world champion in 1991 in single-scull rowing and highly favored to win the event in the upcoming 1992 Olympic games in Barcelona Spain. With the games just 78 days away, Laumann was competing in Essen Germany when another scull rammed into hers. A bone in her right leg was shattered, and a nerve to her foot was cut. Laumann would suffer five operations within the next few weeks. Her doctors said she should recover, but there was no way she could compete in the approaching games. In spite of the advice, Canada did not replace her on the team and almost unbelievably when the Olympic sculling competition began in Barcelona Silken Laumann was there. With the drive that can only be described as Olympian, Laumann limped to her event, cane in hand. And against all the odds, and with what had to be an unbelievable pain, Laumann won the bronze medal. A Canadian journalist would write, "Canada won four gold medals and one bronze medal here today. Let the words go out this day, that the bronze medal shone more brightly in the Barcelona sun than any of the gold."

Teach your kids where they finish does not always measure how far they've come. It is not a question of if they will have to overcome, but when. It is near certain some injury is in their future, some goal will not be reached, or a game will be lost because of their mistake. How they handle small obstacles will aid them in the future with huge ones. You must help them accept what has happened choosing to allow it to build and not break them, just like Takacs and Laumann.

> *"The very problems you must overcome in life also support you and make you stronger in overcoming them." -George Yeoman Pocock in Daniel Brown's The Boys in the Boat.*

The difference between accomplishing and attaining is the personal growth part of the journey to the goal. It's the becoming of something better or greater. All too often we are focused only on the accomplishing, forgetting the power of the becoming part of attainment. Is something happening to them or for them?

Chapter 13

Working With Coaches

A s your children begin to join other kids in sports or competitions, you are forced to share the coaching with others. This can be a time for concern for you. Are you willing to delegate 100% of the mental development of your young performer to another person or persons? How closely should you monitor what is taught to your children? Are there things to watch for in working with coaches?

Coaches Are An Asset

Let's get one thing straight! As long as your children are living at home, you are in charge of their mental skill development. You can ignore this, or not be excellent at it, but you cannot delegate it away. The teachers and coaches at the schools your kids attend get a new group every year to manage. The time they have with them is short and divided by the class or team size. Their positive or negative influence is minor compared to an attentive parent's control.

Teachers and coaches provide the needed skills training that you normally are unable to provide. I am suggesting that you let them provide it with a minimum of interference from you or your spouse. Let them do their job. Your job is to support their coaches and teachers to the benefit of your child.

Be On the Same Page

Family counselors, tend to agree it is critical for your child to see unity between Mom and Dad. You must be on the same page. Conflict creates doubt as to what is the correct thing to believe and do. The same principle applies to the relationship between you and your child's coaches and teachers. If you, for some reason, determine you disagree strongly with the coach, make certain you find common ground by consultation with them or let it go. Under no circumstances should you allow your child to see disunity between the two of you. The last resort is to either fire the coach or leave the program. We train a lot of coaches here at Mental Management Systems who say this is a big problem for them.

Support the Coach

For about 11 years I operated the International Shooting School in Seguin Texas, coaching Olympic hopefuls in International Rifle events. I met privately with every new junior shooter and made them a deal. I promised them, I would never say anything negative about them to any person, including their parents, without first coming to them. I then asked them for the same deal. They agreed, if they had a beef with me, they would come to me first before talking negatively about me to anyone, including their parents. This conversation eliminated almost all conflicts with parents and helped create an optimal relationship between the shooter and the others in our program. I am suggesting you have this kind of a relationship with your coaches and teachers. Your child should never hear you speak negatively about them. You would be furious if a coach made a remark against you to your child. I feel you should offer your coaches the same courtesy.

Choose a Primary-Coach

Some of our junior golf clients have multiple coaches, one for full-swing, one for short game and perhaps a school coach. If you are in a situation similar to this, make certain you select one as the primary-coach. If there is a conflict between two coaches, you must resolve it before confusing your child. Work with the chosen primary coach and have him or her advise your child. You might have to take on the role of primary coach yourself. You should not have two primary coaches at the same time.

Be careful in selecting coaches for your kids. Changing primary-coaches is traumatic in most cases. If your child is fortunate enough to be recruited for a scholarship by a university, the selection of the coach may be critical to the college experience of your young player.

Be Patient With the Coach

After you become familiar with the principles of this book, it is probable you will know more about certain areas of mental coaching than the coach or teacher of your child. If this is the case, do your best to communicate with them without creating an adverse relationship concerning Mental Management issues. Coaches tend to believe the mental game is important but might not have much training in it. You might offer to lend them this book. Be careful; you might not get it back.

Leavers, Leaners, and Leaders

Do you ever wonder why certain high school football programs, cheer teams, band programs, basketball, and hockey teams are always on top? I think one reason is the skill of the coaching staff in developing the Leaners on the team. Organizations such as school teams, classes in school, and virtually any group of people fall into three categories: Leavers, Leaners, and Leaders.

Leavers are going to leave the program. Leaders are going to lead. It will not matter to either of these classifications if the coach is excellent or incompetent. Leaders will lead anyway, and Leavers will leave anyway. The real test of a program is what happens to the Leaners. In an excellent program, the Leaners will lean toward Leading. In a weak program, they will lean toward Leaving. It may be the same with your family.

You might be blessed with a leader. He or she might Lead regardless of the skills of the coaches or teachers in their world right now. You might have a child that for this sport or class, chooses to Leave. It is just not their thing at present, resisting all attempts at helping them to Lead. By the way, there are no Losers. Leavers often become Leaders in time, finding new sports or subjects that turn them on to Leading. That's what happened to me. A genuine test of the skill for you or their coaches will be on how the Leaners in your family lean toward Leading. Leaners make up the vast majority of people. Most of us rarely Lead, occasionally Leave, and most of the time, we are Leaners. God doesn't make Losers, only people who think they are.

Chapter 14

Training Principles

Although you may not be directly overseeing the training of your children, I feel making you aware of fundamental principles we have found useful may help you.

Training or Practice

It is critical your child's understanding of words or concepts are the same as your understanding of them if you desire to maximize helping them with their mental game. Here is an example: I often hear the words training and practice used synonymously. I beg to differ. My dictionary defines training as the action of teaching a person a particular skill or type of behavior. This definition indicates a portion of the performance is isolated and addressed separately. Training is working on the parts of performance.

Practice is simulating the entire performance. When an actor is going over her lines, she is Training. When the entire cast is in a rehearsal of an act, they are Practicing. A dress rehearsal is a Practice of a performance. You do not Train a performance. When a golfer is working on a putting drill on the putting green, he is Training. When he plays a round of golf, he is Practicing. Practicing is simulating under tournament conditions.

Informational or Transformational.

There is a huge difference between knowing something and it becoming like you to do it. Knowing something is Informational while being like you to apply it is Transformational. Reading a book, watching a video, attending a lecture or listening to audio are Informational. Although valuable, these experiences tend to inform but often fall short in changing a person's attitudes or behavior by themselves. For something to become Transformational, four elements are required: Information, Application by an Expert, Confirmation, and Consultation.

A semester in high school can be a Transformational experience for a student. Information is supplied through lecture, reading, watching, and listening. The teacher provides Application by an Expert, Consultation, and Confirmation by interaction individually with a student and corporately with the class. Learning to read, playing an instrument, learning a new language, and playing on a team are examples of Transformational events occurring in school. The teachers and coaches provide Consultation by answering questions and Confirmation through testing and praise.

A big help to parents is to duplicate this process when teaching your children. Just telling them about something is Informational. Parents often expect Transformational results from an Informational investment. Having a Transformational result in mind works well when teaching your kids how to do simple tasks at home. Telling a child, they need to clean their room is Informational, leaving it up to them to determine how to do it. If however, you showed them how you want their room cleaned, you would be in the Application by an Expert phase. Next, observing them cleaning an area provides Confirmation they are doing it correctly. Finally, ask them if they have any questions about the chore, presents an opportunity for Consultation.

You may have to not only inform them, but also guide them in doing the work, confirm they are doing it correctly, and providing counsel when they have questions. Ensuring all four steps are addressed increases the probability they will repeat it successfully in the future.

The Principle of the Break

"People forget what they are doing wrong faster than what they are doing right."

Do you take a break when working? Feels good, doesn't it? Do you look forward to Friday and a break from work? You bet. Taking time off is crucial to developing a consistent mental game. Here are some guidelines.

Training seven days a week will create more problems than it cures, and burn a person out. I do not believe six days a week are better than five. Anything less than five depends on the individual and their circumstances. A break creates an opportunity for rest, reflection, and renewal. Most of my clients report no loss in skill after a break in training. It's not uncommon to discover a surge in ability immediately after one. I believe when on a break we tend to think more about what we need to do than what we have been doing wrong. That's imprinting in the right direction.

The Principle of Focus

"Wherever you are, be all there."-Jim Elliot

My father, a military officer and war hero, had an eighth-grade education, but he was one of the most intelligent men I have known. So, I was a bit surprised when the day before I started college he offered this advice.

"Son, the most important thing about college is going out with girls and having fun. It is more important than making good grades, or shooting winning scores."

"Are you serious?" I asked.

" I am. There will not be another time in your life

where more attractive young women will be available to you. I expect you to enjoy your college years. When you are out with someone you care about, don't think about school or shooting. Focus entirely on your date."

"I can do that," I said

Dad continued. "But, shooting is the most important thing when you are on the range. Do not think about the test you need to pass or who you are going out with tonight while you are training. Do you understand?"

"Sure," I said. But Dad had more to say.

"But, the most important aspect of college is learning something you can use in life when you are in the classroom. While in the class, don't think about shooting, or dating. Listen to the teacher. The most important thing in school is wherever you are, be all there."

Heeding my father's advice would require me to focus on what I was doing at the time, and block out all distractions. I am thankful he did not assume I was practicing this principle.

Progressive Training

The probability of achieving a good result is directly proportional to the difficulty of the task. So, it makes sense to begin every training program with something that is easy, fun to do, and then gradually

increasing the skill level. This method is called Progressive Training. It protects the Self-Image at the
start while improving the confidence and enjoyment
of the participant. Any arduous task can be mastered
if taken in small steps and learned in a progressive
manner. The key to any parent is to help your kids
identify the parts of a task that they feel they have
down. Chances are your children know more than
they think they do. Get them starting with what they
know first, then aid them in advancing toward the
higher skilled areas. One caution here. We seem to
live in a world that has no interest in delayed gratifi-
cation. "Gotta' have it now or forget it." Help them
understand most things of long lasting value do not
come easily or immediately.

Let's look at some examples of starting easy.

Diane starts a putting drill one foot from the hole.
After making ten putts successfully in a row, she
adds a foot to the distance, working her way back to
ten feet.

Jerry is beginning archery lessons. His coach
starts him close to the bale. The target is so big Jerry
rarely misses. Once he has a certain number of successful results in a row, Jerry is moved back, increasing the difficulty. The Self-Image needs positive imprinting in the beginning. If a task seems too difficult
right out of the gate, the performer's interest in the
activity decreases.

Principle of Repetition

"What you do a lot, you become."

In a competition, the number of repetitions is controlled by the rules, but in training, the competitor controls the reps. I recommend helping your children to increase the number of successful attempts while limiting, as best they can, the bad ones.

The athletes in the middle of the leaderboard tend to practice the parts of their game giving them trouble more than what they seem to be doing well. I can relate to this statement. In college, if I performed poorly in a portion of my match I tended to train that stage more often the next week. I soon learned, after making the National Team, the top shooters were doing the opposite.

Olympic Champion Jack Writer told me, "When you are shooting good, shoot a lot. Do not practice losing by only working on your bad shots."

I always began and ended every training session with success. Working on decreasing the mistakes in the previous tournaments was not avoided altogether, but it never exceeded the number of shots trained on what I was doing well. If I had an exceptional performance in training, I always extended the session. If on the other hand, nothing was working I tended to shorten that portion and work on something else or just go home.

The Three Step Training Rule

In Troy Bassham's book *Attainment – The 12 Elements of Elite Performance*, he introduces the Three Step Training Rule. Here is how he describes it.

> Beginning with a favorable outcome is step one. The Self-Image imprints best at the beginning and the end of a training session. Always initiate the training session with a high probability of success. A basketball player working on jump shots starts close to the basket. A musician starts the training session with pieces that are easy to play. A golfer working on putting begins close to the hole. Imprinting success at the outset helps build confidence in the Self-Image for the balance of the session

> The second step is to always work on weak areas of the game in the middle part of the training session. Making sure to start easy and work towards the more challenging areas protects your Self-Image while building the necessary subconscious skills needed to advance.

> The final step is to always end with success. If you're a golfer and putting is the strongest part of your game, then it should be the last thing you practice. This step improves the likelihood of ending on a positive note. The purpose of organizing your training in this manner is to allow for a more effective and

efficient training day.

Start with something easy, then practice the hard stuff, then end on a high is the best way to protect the Self-Image while improving ability. This type of training allows your young performers to do both.

The Mastery Curve

John is on his third day of a major archery competition, and his dad is watching. John is confused and frustrated as he looks at the leaderboard. John shot the best scores of his life on the first day. He tried his best not to change a thing on the second, but his performance on day two was one of the lowest scores he has ever posted. John asks his dad, "What is going on here? I have one more day to shoot. Should I change something?" What would you tell him?

If a performer posts several scores in a row that are among the highest and then follow them with an uncharacteristically low score, he may be a victim of the Mastery Curve Correction Phenomenon. You do not have to be an elite shooter for this to happen, and elite shooters are not immune to its effects. First, let's look at the Mastery Curve.

The Master Curve is a graphical representation of the skill level of a performer. If we progress **at the same rate every time we compete**, our Mastery Curve would be a straight line from our current ability to our goal, as seen in Figure 1.

Figure 1

Performance

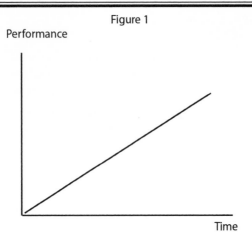

Time

Figure 2

Performance

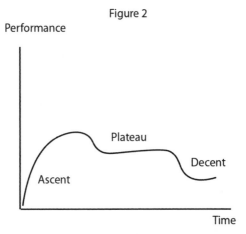

Plateau

Decent

Ascent

Time

But, you and I both know this curve is not straight. In fact, even a world champion's mastery curve has ups and downs just like Figure 2.

If you graph a performer's progress, you will notice periods of success where the performance improves at a rapid rate. This part of the Mastery Curve is called an Ascent. We love Ascents and performers normally do not like to change anything while in one. Not changing anything is the correct thing to do.

We call the period where scores do not go up or down a Plateau and the time when scores are falling a Descent. Performers abhor Plateaus and Descents and the most common remedy chosen to halt one of these periods is to modify something. Now, revision is not always good! Changing to a something new might not be as effective as remaining with the old method. But, young performers tend to think that anything is better than what they are currently doing, so they will change something. Remember, even when we are doing the right thing change takes a toll. Time and effort are needed to implement the change. Now, if the change is unnecessary or perhaps even in the wrong direction a performer can find themselves losing months or maybe years of advancement. Just changing something that does not need changing can cause a Descent.

Now don't get me wrong, if your young performer is actually in a Descent change is exactly what they should do. But, can I offer some suggestions? First, ask them if the error is a result of something they have recently altered. Sometimes it becomes evident they have changed or cut short some element of their mental or technical program, and when they just return to the original pattern of behavior, the problem goes away.

Next, let's be certain they are really on a Descent. Just because performance is dropping does not automatically prove a Descent is occurring. Scores sometimes fall in adverse conditions, when performers are ill or just plain tired. In fact, I know of only one sure way to know if the drop in performance is truly a Descent. Watch if the drop occurs after a Plateau and does not immediately come up. If this occurs, the performer is in a Descent for certain, and they had better change something.

Let's look at one example of when it appears the performer is in a Descent but is not. It is called a Mastery Curve Correction. Simply put, almost every time we experience a sudden surge in scoring (that's an Ascent remember), there is a corresponding temporary correction or downturn in the score at some point. The first time this occurs, I assure you it is a Correction, not a Descent. Let's look at this in Figure 3.

Figure 3

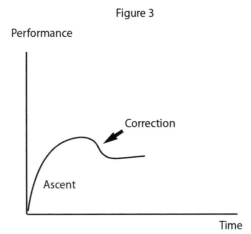

This Performer has just experienced an Ascent followed by a downturn at the point of the arrow. Most players take this result to be a Descent, but it isn't. It's a Self-Image correction, occurring because the Subconscious skill level is growing faster than the Self-Image and the Self-Image corrects the player back to a more believable level. Remember, the Self-Image does not like to change, but the performer is changing. They are getting much better. It is not like them to perform quite this well, so the Self-Image corrects them to a score level that is more like their old performance. Sometimes the score during a Correction is uncharacteristically low, and this is not unusual. When this happens, if the performer does not understand what is going on, they perceive it to be a dramatic Descent, implementing an unwarranted change to stop the bleeding. This action often results in triggering a real Descent, something that does not need to happen.

The appropriate action to take in a Mastery Curve Correction is to return to using the method they were implementing when in the Ascent. Do not deviate from what was working in the Ascent. Soon the performance will begin to improve, and a new Ascent can begin.

Now that you know what to look for the Mastery Curve Correction phenomenon should not take you by surprise and you should be able to nip this problem in the bud for your kids.

Deliberate Training

Two young players on their school's golf team go the course to train. The first one defines a particular goal for the session before starting, isolates an area to work on, and executes repetitive movements to advance skill. The second one drove the ball a little, putted a little, chipped a little and talked to friends. Both of them will say they trained, but only one of them did it deliberately. By the way, there is nothing wrong with the second guy's behavior, as long as he does not care about beating the first.

Deliberate Training includes forming an objective to accomplish, proper mental processing, executing enough repetitions to develop skill, and documenting the improvement. Anything less is just showing up.

Chapter 15

Changing Self-Image

The Self-Image is the total of all of the habits and attitudes of your child. Attitudes determine whether they feel positively or negatively about an item or concept. Habits determine how they behave concerning them. We do certain things because it is consistent with our Self-Image.

Are these attitudes familiar?

"I'm not good at taking tests. I know the answers to the test when I'm studying, but forget them when taking the exam."

"I perform great in practice, but when I get into the competition, my performance drops."

"If I do well at the beginning, I lose it at the end."

"I am not good at speaking in front of people."

"I'm technically sound in my sport, but I choke

under pressure."

These are statements I've heard from students of mine. They are all temporary Self-Image attitudes. They can change. In fact, the same people who held these views initially soon began to talk like this:

"I'm good at taking tests. When I study the material well, I can recall the answers in the exam."

"I perform better in matches than in practice."

"If I start well, I finish well."

"I enjoy speaking before groups."

"I can count on a good performance, especially under pressure."

Self-Image Can Change

What accounted for the change? They all experienced an exchange in Self-Image. Learning to help your children turn negative attitudes into positive ones is an important skill. When the Self-Image changes, performance changes.

Self-Image and Performance Results are Related.

When performer's result is well below their expectation, one place to look for answers is the Self-Image. Performance and Self-Image are almost always equal. If your daughter does not like her score, there is a good chance, for her score to change; her Self-Image needs to change first. The Self-Image resists change, and that's a good thing. If you changed too easily, you would be one person one day and a different one the next. The good news is Self-Image can change, but I admit it is not easy.

Your children know something has to change for their results to improve, but they do not want it to be an internal change in their attitude. They'd prefer to find a solution by having you buy new equipment, send them to a new coach, or simply blame someone else for the problem. They can try the most common method used by frustrated players, that is certain to make them even more frustrated; just train more. That is a good way to change the Subconscious skill, but it will do little to change Self-Image. Practicing more doesn't always improve Self-Image, but Imprinting a good performance always does.

Steps in Changing Self-Image

I believe you can help your young performers change any attitude or habit that is holding them back. You should experience a corresponding change in performance when the Self-Image changes. Here is how to do it in four steps.

1. They Must Be Willing To Change

First, THEY must be willing to change. It may be that YOU desire for your child to change their Self-Image, but they are not onboard with this idea. The Self-Image does not respond to the changes others want us to make. You must help them to decide for themselves. I offer two suggestions. Take advantage of a time when they hit bottom. When things seem to be unable to get worse, kids have a greater appetite to try something you suggest. Secondly, your best leverage with them is THEIR goals. What is important for them? What is the benefit for them to change? If you can get them to admit they are willing to become something new and different, success has a chance.

2. Define the Needed Solution

Next, you must help them identify precisely the habits and attitudes that need to change. Attitudes are opinions believed to be true. There is a good chance a change in their views about their ability to do the task, and a corresponding change in their behavior will be required. Here is a four-step program to get them to define the needed solution.

1. Get them to choose a goal to attain.

I am an A student in math.

2. Ask them to think of someone they know who is already there. We will call him an Expert.

John is an A student.

3. Ask them to list the habits and attitudes of the Expert. Your child talks to John asking him why he is so good at math.

> *John always does his homework in math*
> *when he first gets home from school. He*
> *looks over his homework, selecting example*

problems that might be on the test, prepares
a sample exam and studies it the night be-
fore the exam. John always says he is good
in math when I talk to him

4. Finally, ask them to identify how they differ
from the Expert. What do they have to change about
themselves to become like the Expert?

I like to watch TV a little before I do my
homework. I just study the book the night
before the exam. I often comment math is
not my thing.

3. Identify a New Self-Image

Third, you must identify a new Self-Image that
is in direct conflict with their old one. For example,

I am good in math. I always do my home-
work in math when I first get home from
school. I look over my homework, selecting
example problems that might be on the test,
prepare a sample exam and study it the night
before the exam. I always say I am good in
math when talking to others.

4. Swap the Old For the New

Fourth, help them exchange the old Self-Image
for the desired one by only Imprinting the new attitude or habit and trying to eliminate Imprinting the
old one.

Tell them, "Your Self-Image is the CURRENT
state of YOU. It is not the FINAL state. Be aware that
your Self-Image is evolving in the direction of your
Imprinting. The better you control your Imprinting,

the greater the success in everything you attempt."

Let's Look at Another Example.

Donny was an excellent young basketball player who had a chance to make his school's starting squad. His defensive ability was solid. He was a good shooter, but his percentage at the free-throw line was weak. So poor in fact, the coach hesitated to play him in critical situations. The coach knew that Donny's deficiency was a mental attitude about the free-throw line. When Donny's dad questioned him about his not starting, Donny would say, "I can make free-throws better than anyone on the team in practice, but I just don't shoot free-throws well in a game. I never have." With that attitude, Donny had no chance to start. Also, his Dad notices Donny has a bad habit of getting mad when missing a free-throw in a game, thereby reinforcing his error. Donny needs to change his Self-Image from "I am a bad free-throw shooter in a game" to "I am the best free-throw shooter on the team."

One day Donny approached the coach.

"I'm ready to do whatever it takes to make the starting squad. What do I have to do?"

"Donny, you have all the skills required to start on our team. But, your performance at the foul line in a game must improve for that to happen. I've seen you make free-throws in practice, so I know your technique is not the issue. For some reason, you have lost your confidence, and you must find a way to get it back."

Donny's father picks him up after practice, and they begin talking about what the coach said.

"Donny, are you thinking the same things before and after a free-throw in a game that you do in practice?"

"Yes and no. I think the same things before the shot every time in both training and a game, but I tend to get upset when I miss."

"I can help you fix your free-throws if you are willing to change one attitude and one habit. Are you ready to do that?"

"Sure, but how do I know what habit and attitude need changing?"

"It is easier than you think. Just look at the problems you are having and start there. If you turn your weaknesses into strengths, your performance will surely benefit. The attitude that needs changing is your opinion of yourself that you are not a good free-throw shooter. Would believing you were one of the best free-throw shooters on the team, cause you to improve your percentage on the line?"

"Sure."

"Then, all you have to do is change your attitude about making free-throws. The view you currently have is not based on your skill; it is based on your Imprinting. You have too many Imprints of 'It's not like me to make free-throws in a game' in your Self-Image. You need to replace Imprinting what you are doing wrong with doing it right. That's how you change Self-Image. Are you willing to do that?"

"Yes, I want to change my Self-Image but how do I do it?"

"Begin by responding to the shots you attempt in a game instead of reacting to them. When you make a free-throw, reinforce it. Picture it again in your mind, then say to yourself, "That's like me!" When you miss a shot, immediately think, "What do I need to do to make it next time?" Then let it go. Put it out of your mind. Even the pros miss a few free-throws."

"Is that all I have to do?"

"Almost. Remember, your Self-Image imprints most immediately after the shot. Your old habits of getting mad and beating yourself up with every miss increase the probability of missing in the future. Your Self-Image is like a container holding all of the imprints. You need to picture more hits than misses. That's the key. If you rehearse making the shot before and after an attempt, your Self-Image cannot shrink. Only think about what you want to happen when you are off of the court. Reinforce your successes and learn from your failures. That's all you have to do."

Learning From the Example

The previous illustration addresses the two of the most common errors made by young performers; Reacting negatively to a poor result and failing to reinforce the Self-Image positively when the result is good.

Kids struggle with this one every time they fail to win. In the reinforcement phase of an action, the performer must determine the best course of action for the next attempt. Teach them not to be afraid of making mistakes. John Maxwell once wrote, "The greatest mistake we make is living in constant fear that we will make one." If your kids are fearful of making mistakes their focus in a competition is on the outcome, not on execution, and their mental game will always be a variable. When their focus is on avoiding error, the picture they are imprinting on their Self-Image is the error itself. Ninety percent of everything we worry about never happens, and even when it does, many times it is for our benefit.

> *"If you do not teach your children to view failure as a lesson, they will see themselves as failures."*

Chapter 16
If I Were Your Kid.

"I would want you to care about what I care about, even if you do not care about it."

*"I would want you to **inform** me when I need to know **what** to do - **teach** me when I need to know **how** to do it - **motivate** me by telling me **why** I am doing it - **remember to praise me** when I do it well."*

"I would want you to help me find something I can learn to do better than my peers to enhance my Self-Image."

"I would want you to teach me that Obstacles are Opportunities."

"I would want you to help me to picture what I want to happen and not what I am afraid might happen."

"I would want you to reinforce my successes and always help me to forget my failures."

"I would want you to cheer for me when I succeed and help me learn when I don't."

"I would want you to tell me what I need to do, not just what I did wrong."

"I would want you to ask me what I did right when you first talk to me after I perform."

"I would want you to care more about who I am becoming than what I am accomplishing."

"I would want you to be patient when I struggle, encourage me when I stumble, and pick me up me when I'm down."

"I would want you to see me as valuable when others discard me."

"I would want you to hold me when I hurt."

"I would want you to correct me when you see I am wrong."

"I would want you to praise me when you see I'm right."

"I would want you to dislike my bad behavior, but let me know you still like me."

"I would want you always to be someone I can talk to about anything."

"I would want you to be a worthy example for me to follow."

'I would want you to have my back and always be there for me."

Thank you for reading Parenting Champions. If you would like to be kept informed about additional ways to help you apply the information in this book, or would like a copy of our recommended book reading list, please send us an email at info@mentalmanagement.com, and we will add you to our free monthly newsletter.

Lanny Bassham, founder of Mental Management® Systems, is the driving force behind the creation of the mental strategies presented in the seminars and products offered by the company.

Lanny not only developed the Mental Management® System but also used it personally to win 35 medals in international rifle competition for the USA including 22 world individual and team titles, setting 4 world records and winning the coveted Olympic Gold Medal in Montreal in 1976. This ranks him third in medal count for the USA among all shooters. Lanny is a member of the USA Shooting Hall of Fame. He lives in Frisco, Texas.

Hear Lanny Bassham at your event.

Keynote Speeches include:

What Parents Need to Know about the Mental Game. *- The most important mental coach in every athlete's life is the parent that drives them home from the game. Parents are unprepared for the job, and though they love their children, they will likely do more harm than good as their mental coach.*

When Silver is Not Enough *- Lanny's personal story of the boy who couldn't make the team, and was picked last in every sport to become an Olympic Champion. Throughout the story of his life Lanny tells several principles of success that can be applied to any business situation.*

Freedom Flight *- a message on controlling your mind in spite of your environment. This story is based on a true event where Lanny met someone who changed his life and direction forever. This story is also available in book or audio CD.*

To learn more about how Mental Management® can help you in your sport or business please call 972-899-9640 or you may also send an email to info@mentalmanagement. com and we will be happy to assist you.

What If High School Students Knew
What the Winners Know?

Every high school in the country has teachers and coaches that prepare students to acquire a skill. That is important. But the winners all say that the WAY YOU THINK is 90% of WINNING, and there are no courses in school to prepare the students in this 90%. What if such a course existed?

95% of winning is accomplished by 5% of the participants. Lanny Bassham has spent his career studying and teaching the top 5%. One fact stands out; the winners are thinking differently than those in the middle of the leaderboard, and this information is not made available to your children in school.

The remark he hears from his students most often is "I wish I'd had this information sooner." Now, Bassham's company, Mental Management® Systems has developed a course called WHAT THE WINNERS KNOW for high school students.

Imagine being able to take a course in high school designed to prepare students with principles, tools and techniques developed and used by Olympic champions, to think like the top 5% and apply this knowledge to academics, school sports, and a future vocation.

How the Program Works

Using the same slides and concepts Lanny Bassham uses to teach his students, Mental Management® Systems has developed a semester-long curriculum for high school students. Students will receive student packets consisting of a Student Handbook, the books *With Winning in Mind, Attainment, Freedom Flight*, and a Performance Journal.

WHAT THE WINNERS KNOW

What Your Children Will Learn

Why 95% of Winning is Accomplished by only 5% of the Participants | What to Think About Before a Big Test | How to Respond Instead of React To a Mistake or Failed Attempt | 3 Attitudes the Top 5% Possess that Keep Them on Top | # 1 Reason Why Skilled Performers Fail in Competition | How the Reinforcement Phase Affects the Self-Image | The Difference Between Life Purpose and Life Goals | How to Turn Off Distraction and Study Effectively | The Mental Management® Goal Setting System | 3 Mental Processes that Control Performance | Why Our Beliefs about Pressure are Myths | Six Principles of Mental Management® | Why Giving it 110% Doesn't Work | 12 Strategies to Control Pressure | How to Change Self-Image | How to Set the Right Goal | How to Stay Motivated | Three Phases of a Goal | The Keys to Consistency | How to Turn Off Distraction and Study Effectively | The Difference Between Deliberate Training and Wasting Time | How to Overcome Obstacles and Turn Them Into Opportunities | How to Stop Worrying About a Failure in the Future | Learn What to Think About Before, During, and After a Task | How to Protect Your Self-Image From Negative People | Learn the Same Mental System Olympic Champions Use to Win the Gold.

For information to add "WHAT THE WINNERS KNOW" to your child's high school call 972-899-9640.

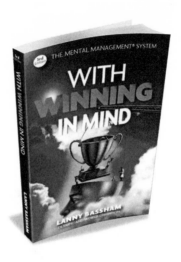

WITH WINNING IN MIND

The book that started it all, great for anyone interested in having a consistent mental performance under pressure. The book introduces Mental Management© and is packed with techniques for competitors. Learn how performance is a function of three mental processes, how to control the mind under pressure and how to train for competition. Unlock the secrets of Olympic Champions.

Order at 972-899-9640
www.mentalmanagementstore.com

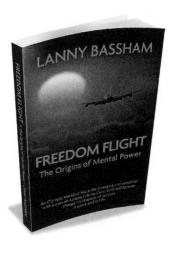

FREEDOM FLIGHT

The Origins of Mental Power

Olympic Silver Medalist, Lanny Bassham, was feeling truly defeated and sorry for himself due to his failure to reach his ultimate goal. He meets a man who changes his perspective, his attitude and most importantly his future. An unlikely mentor named Jack explains to Lanny that he is has lost his freedom, and is living in a self-imposed prison. During their plane flight to Cairo, these two strangers embark on a truly inspirational discovery. Inspired by true events this 96 page book includes 14 success principles and packs a powerful punch to those who choose to experience the flight of their life. Take back your freedom, break down the walls to your self-imposed prison and reach for your dreams.

Order at 972-899-9640
www.mentalmanagementstore.com